# TOP 10 ISTANBUL

MELISSA SHALES

EYEWITNESS TRAVEL

Left **Gate of Felicity, Topkapı Palace** Centre **Mehter Band** Right **Blue Mosque**

LONDON, NEW YORK,
MELBOURNE, MUNICH AND DELHI
www.dk.com

Produced by Coppermill Books
55 Salop Road, London E17 7HS

Printed and bound in China by Leo Paper Products Ltd

First American Edition, 2007

13 14 15 16 10 9 8 7 6 5 4 3 2 1

Published in the United States by
DK Publishing, 375 Hudson Street,
New York, New York 10014

**Reprinted with revisions 2009, 2011, 2013**



Published in Great Britain by Dorling Kindersley Limited.

A catalog record is available from the Library of Congress.

ISSN 1479-344X

ISBN: 978-0-75669-666-5

Within each Top 10 list in this book, no hierarchy of quality or popularity is implied. All 10 are, in the editor's opinion, of roughly equal merit.

Floors are referred to throughout in accordance with British usage; ie the "first floor" is the floor above ground level.

# Contents

## Istanbul's Top 10



**The information in this DK Eyewitness Top 10 Travel Guide is checked regularly.**
Every effort has been made to ensure that this book is as up-to-date as possible at the time of going to press. Some details, however, such as telephone numbers, opening hours, prices, gallery hanging arrangements and travel information are liable to change. The publishers cannot accept responsibility for any consequences arising from the use of this book, nor for any material on third party websites, and cannot guarantee that any website address in this book will be a suitable source of travel information. We value the views and suggestions of our readers very highly. Please write to: Publisher, DK Eyewitness Travel Guides, Dorling Kindersley, 80 Strand, London WC2R 0RL, Great Britain, or email: travelguides@dk.com.

Cover: Front – **4Corners:** SIME/Anna Serrano main; **DK Images:** Tony Souter bl. Spine – **DK Images:** Linda Whitwam b. Back – **DK Images:** Tony Souter tl; Linda Whitwam tc; Francesca Yorke tr.

Left **Grand Bazaar** Centre **Dolmabahçe Palace** Right **View from Sülemaniye Mosque**

Left **Deesis Mosaic, South Gallery, Haghia Sophia** Right **Fortress of Asia**

# ISTANBUL'S TOP 10



ISTANBUL'S TOP 10

# TOP 10 Highlights of Istanbul

*Istanbul is one of the greatest cities the world has ever known. Inhabited for at least 5,000 years, it was capital of two of the world's most powerful empires – those of the Byzantines and the Ottomans – and its every stone is steeped in history. The highlights are easy; you can cover the major attractions in the first couple of days. But after that, the choice can be overwhelming, especially as this ancient city is reinventing itself once more as a modern centre for nightlife, food and shopping. The only answer is to come back again – and again. If you do, this endlessly fascinating city will certainly reward you.*

### 1 Topkapı Palace

A palace fit for a sultan, several wives, hundreds of concubines and thousands of retainers, the Topkapı was not only a royal residence, but also the Ottoman Empire's centre of government *(see pp8–11)*.

### 2 Haghia Sophia

One of the greatest icons of the Christian church, Haghia Sophia has stood for 1,500 years – a miraculous feat of design and engineering that has survived fire, war and earthquake, and outlived two great empires *(see pp12–13)*.

### 3 Blue Mosque

Sultan Ahmet I's great mosque is one of the world's most famous religious buildings – "blue" on account of the delicately patterned İznik tiles which adorn the interior *(see pp14–15)*.

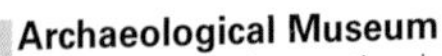

### 4 Archaeological Museum

Turkey's world-class national collection, which remarkably was begun only in the mid-19th century, contains ancient treasures from across the length and breadth of the Ottoman Empire and beyond, including artifacts from Babylon, Syria, Egypt, Greece, Rome and Persia *(see pp16–17)*.

### 5 Grand Bazaar

More mall than market since its last restoration, the Grand Bazaar remains a true Turkish delight, a shopaholic's colourful fantasy that is also a photographer's dream. Whether you are after a Hereke carpet or a pair of silk slippers, you will be satisfied here – in the bazaar at the western end of the Silk Road *(see pp18–19)*.

Preceding pages **Exterior view of the Blue Mosque**

## 6 Süleymaniye Mosque

Sultan Süleyman I, the Ottomans' greatest emperor, and Sinan, the empire's most talented architect, created more than 400 buildings together. This imposing mosque is their masterwork *(see pp20–21)*.

## 7 Church of St Saviour in Chora

With more than 100 profoundly beautiful early-14th-century mosaics and frescoes of biblical scenes, this church is one of the greatest of Istanbul's many Byzantine treasures *(see pp22–3)*.

## 8 Çemberlitaş Baths

The perfect way to recuperate from an overdose of sightseeing is to steam gently beneath the marble domes of a traditional Turkish bath before allowing an attendant to massage those aching feet. The experience is cleansing, cultural and reviving *(see pp24–5)*.

## 10 Bosphorus Cruise

Take to the water on a ferry trip up the Bosphorus, and enjoy a fabulously lazy day off. The air is clean, the pace unhurried and, best of all, sightseeing can be done from the deck, with the promise of a great lunch ahead *(see pp28–9)*.

## 9 Dolmabahçe Palace

This 19th-century Occidental fantasy was a key component in the downfall of the Ottoman Empire. Sultan Abdül Mecit's decision to build a lavishly opulent European-style palace almost bankrupted the Treasury, and in the end could be financed only by foreign loans *(see pp26–7)*.

# Topkapı Palace

*Fresh from his conquest of Constantinople, Mehmet II built Topkapı Sarayı as his main residence in 1459–65. He planned it as a series of pavilions in four courtyards – a tribute in stone to the tent encampments of his nomadic forebears. Mehmet's palace was also the seat of government, and contained a college for training officials and soldiers. While government moved across the road to the Sublime Porte in the 16th century, Topkapı continued as the sultan's palace until Abdül Mecit I moved to Dolmabahçe Palace in 1856.*

*Imperial Gate*

**Book your ticket for the Harem as soon as you arrive, and see the rest of the palace while waiting for your time-slot.**

**There is a café in the first courtyard and a good (if expensive) restaurant, Konyalı, for lunch in the fourth. This is a good place to try Ottoman court cuisine, but it can be crowded. You can book a table in advance on (0212) 513 96 96.**

- *Babıhümayun Cad*
- *Map S3*
- *(0212) 512 04 80*
- *Open 9am–5pm (7pm in summer) Wed–Mon*
- *25 TL plus an additional 15 TL for entry to the Harem (tickets are available at the kiosk by the Harem entrance)*
- *www.topkapisarayi.gov.tr*

## Top 10 Features

1. Imperial Gate
2. First Courtyard
3. Harem
4. Gate of Salutations
5. Kitchens
6. Throne Room
7. Third Courtyard
8. Imperial Wardrobe
9. Treasury
10. Imperial Sofa

### 1 Imperial Gate (Bâb-ı Hümayun)

Built in 1478, this gate *(above left)* is the main entrance to the palace, with gatekeepers' quarters on either side. An apartment belonging to Mehmet II above the gate was destroyed by fire in 1866.

### 2 First Courtyard (Alay Meydanı)

This vast outer courtyard takes in all of Gülhane Park, sweeping down the hill to Sirkeci and including the 6th-century church of Haghia Eirene (Aya İrini Kilisesi), the wooden houses of Soğukçeşme Sokağı and the imposing Archaeological Museum.

### 3 Harem

A maze of rooms and corridors, the Harem was a closed world occupied by the sultan's wives, concubines and children. A guided tour is a must.

### 4 Gate of Salutations (Bâb-üs Selâm)

At this elaborate gate *(left)*, built in 1524, visitors were greeted, and high officials who had upset the sultan were arrested and strangled. The gateway leads into the Second Courtyard (Divan Meydanı), where the Treasury now has a magnificent display of arms and armour.

*Don't miss the fascinating collection of priceless miniatures and manuscripts situated next to the Treasury.*

### 5 Kitchens

These huge kitchens once catered for 800–1,000 people a day. Now they display a marvellous collection of ceramics, crystal and silver, including the Chinese celadon ware favoured by early sultans because, supposedly, it changed colour when it came into contact with poison.

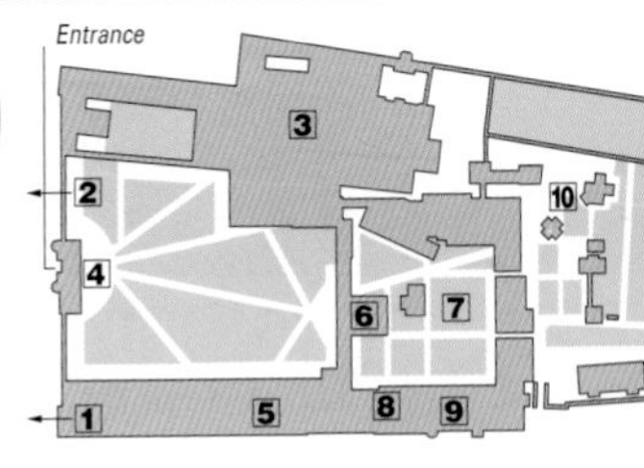

### 6 Throne Room (Arz Odası)

In the Throne Room *(right)*, the Sultan would consult his ministers and governors, welcome ambassadors and other dignitaries, and host smaller formal state occasions.

### 7 Third Courtyard (Enderûn Meydanı)

The Gate of Felicity (Bâb-üs Saadet) leads to the Third Courtyard, containing the sultan's private quarters and those of the Harem's white eunuchs.

### 8 Imperial Wardrobe (Seferli Koğuşu)

Fittingly, the Imperial Wardrobe is now the home of the costume museum, a sumptuous collection of some 3,000 elaborately embroidered royal robes *(above)*.

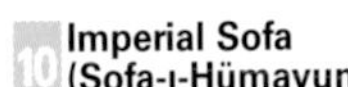

### 9 Treasury (Hazine Koğuşu)

With exhibits including the jewel-encrusted Topkapı Dagger *(below)* and the amazing 86-carat Spoonmaker's Diamond, the Topkapı Treasury may be the most ostentatious collection of wealth ever gathered outside of the legendary Aladdin's cave.

### 10 Imperial Sofa (Sofa-ı-Hümayun)

The Imperial Sofa was a place to relax, its gardens studded with pavilions built by successive sultans. The finest is the Baghdad Pavilion (Bağdat Köşkü), built by Murat IV in 1639 to celebrate his capture of the city of Baghdad the year before.

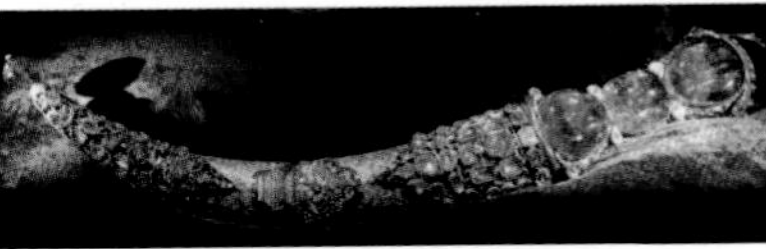

### Religious Relics

The Pavilion of the Holy Mantle (Hasoda Koğuşu) contains several of Islam's holiest relics. Exhibits include hairs from the Prophet's beard, one of his teeth, two of his swords and the sacred standard used during his military campaigns. The most important relic of all is the Holy Mantle, a plain black camel-hair cloak that the Prophet gave as a present to a poet. Once a year, it was displayed to high officials then doused in water; the drops squeezed from it were sent out as talismans against the plague.

*The Pavilion of the Holy Mantle, in the Third Courtyard, is an important pilgrimage site and should be treated with respect.*

Left **Imperial Baths** Centre **Salon of the Valide Sultan** Right **Imperial Hall**

# TOP 10 Features of the Topkapı Harem

### 1 Barracks of the Black Eunuchs

Apart from the sultan and his sons, the only men allowed into the Harem were the black eunuchs, up to 200 slaves from Sudan and Ethiopia. Their barracks lie on one side of the Courtyard of the Black Eunuchs, with its arcade of marble columns.

### 2 Courtyard of the Concubines

This colonnaded courtyard lies beside the Harem Baths. As many as 300 concubines lived in the Harem at a time.

### 3 Golden Cage

Mehmet III became sultan in 1595, following the murder of all but one of his 19 brothers. After that, heirs to the throne were kept in the "Golden Cage", a secure area of the Harem, until they were needed. As a result, many were weak, feeble-minded, and certainly ill-fitted for government when they took the throne.

**Courtyard of the Black Eunuchs**

**Detail, the Golden Cage**

### 4 Salon of the Valide Sultan

The valide sultan (sultan's mother) was by far the most powerful woman in the palace, and enjoyed the use of some of the best rooms in the Harem.

### 5 Sultan's Apartments

The sultan spent much of his off-duty time in his suite within the Harem. Look out for the gilded bedroom of Sultan Abdül Hamit I (1774–89), the Hall of Murat III (1574–95), and the beautiful Fruit Room *(see p58)*.

### 6 Imperial Baths

Standing next to each other at the centre of the complex are the baths of the sultan and the valide sultan, both elegantly faced with marble.

### 7 Imperial Hall

In the Imperial Hall the sultan entertained his closest friends. Although the hall was within the Harem, only a few women – the sultan's mother, chief wife, favourites and daughters – were allowed entry.

### 8 Favourites' Apartments

*Haseki* (favourites) who bore a child received their own apartments and their freedom (if slaves). After the sultan's death, those who had borne only daughters were married out of the Harem or moved to the old palace, while those with sons remained in the palace.

*The guided tour of the Harem is extensive, covering around 40 rooms.*

## 9 Wives' Apartments

The sultan's wives (under Islamic law, he was allowed to have up to four) also had their own apartments. While wives took formal precedence in the Harem hierarchy, the real power lay with the sultan's favourites and mother. Occasionally a sultan would marry a concubine – as in the case of Süleyman I, who married his beloved Roxelana (known in Turkish as Haseki Hürrem). Wives were often traded in political treaties.

## 10 Golden Way

This long, dark passage is known as the Golden Way because on festivals the Sultan would scatter gold coins here for the members of the Harem.

### Top 10 Ottoman Women

1. Hafsa Sultan (mother of Süleyman I)
2. Roxelana (wife of Süleyman)
3. Nurbanu Sultan (wife of Selim II, daughter-in-law of Süleyman)
4. Mihrimah (daughter of Süleyman, wife of Grand Vizier Rüstem Paşa)
5. Safiye Sultan (mother of Mehmet III)
6. Handan Sultan (wife of Mehmet III)
7. Kösem Sultan (wife of Ahmet I)
8. Hatice Turhan Sultan (mother of Mehmet IV)
9. Nakşidil Sultan (mother of Mahmut II)
10. Bezmiâlem (wife of Mahmut II, mother of Abdül Mecit I)

Roxelana

## Life in the Harem

*Behind the doors of the Harem, life was far less exciting than it was portrayed to be in the breathless accounts of 19th-century European commentators. There was undoubtedly intrigue, and if a woman was fortunate enough to be one of the sultan's favourites she might well develop a taste for lavish comfort and lovely gifts, yet daily existence for most was mundane – even dully routine. The Harem was less a den of vice than a family home and girls' school. Of its 1,000 or so occupants, more than two-thirds were servants or royal children, while concubines – who usually arrived between the ages of 5 and 12 – spent years living in dormitories and undergoing a thorough education before being introduced to the sultan.*

***The Favourite Sultana*** **by Etienne Jeaurat – a European vision of Harem life.**

*The English word harem derives from the Arabic* harām *("forbidden").*

# TOP 10 Haghia Sophia

*Haghia Sophia, the Church of Holy Wisdom (Ayasofya in Turkish), is an awe-inspiring expression of religious faith and one of the world's foremost architectural wonders. The first church on the site burned down in 404, the second was destroyed during the Nika Riots of 532, but the third – inaugurated by Emperor Justinian in 537 – stands firm today, despite countless wars and earthquakes, a blazing beacon to the faith of its creators. The church was converted into a mosque in 1453. Since 1934 it has been a museum.*

*Imperial Box*

**After your visit, it's well worth coming back at night to see both Haghia Sophia and the Blue Mosque floodlit.**

**No refreshments are provided within the complex, but there are many options in Sultanahmet Square and Divanyolu Caddesi, a couple of minutes' walk away.**

- *Sultanahmet Meydanı*
- *Map R4*
- *(0212) 528 45 00*
- *Open 9am–6pm Tue–Sun in summer, 9:30am–4:30pm Tue–Sun in winter*
- *Adm 25 TL*
- *www.ayasofyamuzesi.gov.tr*

## Top 10 Features

1. Exterior
2. Galleries
3. Weeping Pillar
4. Columns
5. Narthex
6. Coronation Square
7. Islamic Elements
8. Nave
9. Dome
10. Windows

### 1 Exterior

Its deep red walls piled high with semidomes soaring up towards the vast central dome, the main building is much as it was in the 6th century – except for the buttresses added to secure the structure, which, unfortunately, partly obscure the original shape.

### 2 Galleries

Women used the galleries for prayer. There are splendid mosaics in the south gallery: look out for Christ Pantocrator (Almighty) with John the Baptist and the Virgin Mary; and Mary holding the Infant Christ, flanked by Emperor John II Comnenus and Empress Irene *(below)*.

### 3 Weeping Pillar

Emperor Justinian rested his aching head against the damp stone of this pillar *(above)* and was instantly cured. Ever since, visitors have queued to touch the miraculous spot.

### 4 Columns

The Byzantines were great scavengers, and most of the columns in the Haghia Sophia were salvaged from pagan temples.

*The architects who created Haghia Sophia were two Greek mathematicians, Isidorus of Miletus and Anthemius of Tralles.*

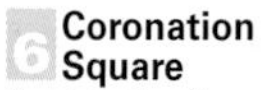

## 5 Narthex

There are doors leading into the nave from each bay of the narthex; the large central one, the Imperial Gate, was once reserved for the Emperor and the Patriarch. At the south end of the narthex, look back above the door as you exit into the Vestibule of the Warriors to see the wonderful 6th-century mosaic of Constantine and Justinian offering their city and church to the infant Christ *(above)*.

## 6 Coronation Square

Set into the floor near the *minbar*, the site of the emperor's throne is marked in a square of patterned marble. In Byzantine times, this was considered to be the centre of the world (*omphalion*).

## 7 Islamic Elements

The conversion of the church into a mosque began in 1453. The mosaics were plastered over (and discovered only in the 1930s). The *mihrab* and *minbar* *(see p15)* were added by Sultan Murat III in the 16th century. Look up to see the calligraphic roundels *(above)* at the base of the dome.

## 8 Nave

On entering the nave *(below)* the overwhelming impression is of the vast space enclosed by the dome. This sits on four arches rising out of four enormous marble piers, which frame double colonnades at either end.

## 9 Dome

The soaring dome, 32 m (101 ft) in diameter, rises 56 m (183 ft) above the ground. Supported by 40 ribs made from special lightweight hollow bricks, it was and remains a miracle of engineering. The original design was even more ambitious – it survived for 21 years before being destroyed by an earthquake in 559.

## 10 Windows

Banks of windows in the tympanum walls beneath the dome, as well as a circle of windows between the ribs of the dome, flood the church with light.

### Changing Faces

In the last bay of the south gallery, on the east wall, look for the superb mosaic of Christ enthroned, flanked by Empress Zoë and Emperor Constantine IX Monomachus. It is clear that the emperor's head has been altered. Historians believe that the figure was initially a portrait of Zoë's first husband, Romanos III Argyros, but after his death in 1034 it was replaced with the image of her second husband, Michael IV. After Michael died in 1041, the face of her third husband, Constantine, was added.

# TOP 10 Blue Mosque

*Sultan Ahmet I was only 19 when he commissioned this superb mosque, known in Turkish as the Sultanahmet Camii. So great was his enthusiasm for the project that at times he even worked alongside his labourers. With his architect, Mehmet Ağa, he wanted to surpass the Süleymaniye Mosque (the work of Ağa's teacher, Sinan) and Haghia Sophia. The result of their labours, completed in 1616, has become one of the most celebrated mosques in the world, known widely as the Blue Mosque because of the blue İznik tiles in the interior.*

*Prayer time*

**To avoid prayer times, make the mosque your first stop in the morning, or visit in the mid-afternoon.**

**There are no places for refreshment inside the mosque complex, but Sultanahmet Square, Divanyolu Caddesi and the Arasta Bazaar offer plenty of possibilities.**

- *Sultanahmet Meydanı*
- *Map R5*
- *(0212) 518 13 19*
- *Open 9am–7pm daily, except during prayers*
- *Donations*
- *May–Sep: son-et-lumière performances each evening, with Turkish, English, French and German on different nights. Free*

## Top 10 Features

1. The Setting
2. Entrance
3. Domes
4. Minarets
5. Ablutions Fountain
6. Courtyard
7. Tiles
8. Minbar and Mihrab
9. Sultan's Loge
10. Carpets

### 1 The Setting

To underline the supremacy of Islam over Christian Byzantium, the Blue Mosque was built opposite Haghia Sophia *(above)*, on the site of the Byzantine royal palace.

### 2 Entrance

The monumental main entrance to the mosque is rarely used. There are separate entrances for those going to pray and for tourists, around the side of the courtyard.

### 3 Domes

Semidomes *(right)* surround the main dome, which is 23.5 m (77 ft) in diameter and 43 m (140 ft) high, and supported by four giant columns, each 5 m (16 ft) in diameter.

### 4 Minarets

Legend has it that the sultan asked for a minaret capped with *altın* (gold), but the architect thought he had asked for *altı* (six) minarets. The sultan was pleased – no mosque apart from the great mosque in Mecca had six minarets.

*Try to see the mosque by night at least once – it is beautiful at any time, but especially so when floodlit.*

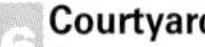

## 5 Ablutions Fountain

The fountain *(left)* at the centre of the mosque's courtyard is no longer used for ritual ablutions. Instead, the faithful use taps ranged along the outside of the courtyard. Washing the face, arms, neck, feet, mouth and nose is seen as an integral part of the act of prayer.

## 6 Courtyard

The huge courtyard, which is faced with cool marble from the island of Marmara, has the same dimensions as the interior of the prayer hall. Look up for a splendid view of the mosque's cascade of domes and semidomes.

## 7 Tiles

The majority of the blue İznik tiles *(above)* that give the mosque its name are too high on the interior walls to examine in detail. There are 20,143 tiles of 70 different styles – fulfilling the order put severe pressure on the İznik tile makers, and the sultan banned anyone else from placing orders until his was complete.

## 8 Minbar and Mihrab

At the front of the mosque are the *minbar (left)*, the pulpit from which the imam delivers his sermons, and the *mihrab (below)*, a niche that points towards Mecca.

## 9 Sultan's Loge

To the left of the *mihrab* is the galleried box where the sultan prayed, its ceiling painted with arabesque designs.

## 10 Carpets

The whole of the interior is laid with a modern carpet. Mosques have always had carpets, to cushion the knees and forehead during prayers.

### İznik Tiles

Ceramic production in İznik began during the Byzantine era. In the early years, the designs were based on Chinese models. Arabic motifs were added by Şah Kulu, one of 16 artists brought in from Tabriz by Sultan Selim I (1512–20). A rich turquoise was added to the traditional blue and white in the 1530s; purples, greens and coral reds came 20 years later. Master designer Kara Memi introduced swirling floral patterns, and by the time Ahmet I placed his order for the Blue Mosque, the İznik style was established.

For tips on Islamic etiquette **See p39**

# TOP 10 Archaeological Museum

*The national collection of one of the world's most ancient and enthralling countries naturally promises something special, and this fabulous museum does not disappoint. A world-class collection spanning 5,000 years, it was founded in 1881 by Osman Hamdi Bey, the son of a grand vizier, fuelled by the realization that European archaeologists and treasure-hunters were walking off with much of the Empire's heritage. There are three sections: the main museum, the Tiled Pavilion (Çinili Köşk) and the Museum of the Ancient Orient.*

*Façade*

**It is not unusual to find some galleries closed due to staff shortages.**

**There is a fairly rudimentary drinks kiosk in the grounds.**

- *Osman Hamdi Bey Yokuşu, Topkapı Sarayı, Gülhane*
- *Map S3*
- *(0212) 520 77 40*
- *Open 9am–6pm Tue–Sun*
- *Adm 10 TL*
- *www.istanbularkeoloji.gov.tr*

## Top 10 Features

1. Sidon Sarcophagi
2. Alexander Sarcophagus
3. Ishtar Gate
4. Hattuşaş Sphinx
5. Halikarnassos Lion
6. Treaty of Kadesh
7. Museum of the Ancient Orient
8. Tiled Pavilion
9. Istanbul Through the Ages
10. Anatolia and Troy Gallery

### 1 Sidon Sarcophagi

Osman Hamdi Bey discovered this remarkable group of 5th- and 4th-century-BC sarcophagi *(below)* in Sidon (modern Lebanon) in 1887.

### 2 Alexander Sarcophagus

Its high-relief frieze shows scenes of Alexander victorious in battle against the Persians, but the Alexander Sarcophagus, dating from the late 4th century BC, is in fact the tomb of King Abdalonymos of Sidon (died c. 312 BC). Faint traces remain of the gaudy colour that would once have covered it.

### 3 Ishtar Gate

The Ishtar Gate, built by King Nebuchadnezzar in 575 BC, was decorated with mosaic ceramic panels of dragons and bulls *(main image)*. The Processional Way through the gate was lined with 120 lions.

### 4 Hattuşaş Sphinx

This enigmatic 13th-century-BC stone feline was one of four discovered in the great Hittite city at Hattuşaş (Boğazkale) in Anatolia.

### 5 Halikarnassos Lion

The tomb of King Mausolus was one of the seven wonders of the ancient world – this simple lion *(left)* is a surviving relic.

*The tomb of Mausolus was so magnificent that his name has been enshrined for posterity in the word "mausoleum".*

## 6 Treaty of Kadesh

The world's oldest surviving peace treaty *(below)*, carved in stone in 1269 BC, was agreed by Egyptian Pharoah Ramses II and King Muwatalli of the Hittites after a battle in present-day Syria. It lays out the terms of the ceasefire and agrees the safe return of refugees.

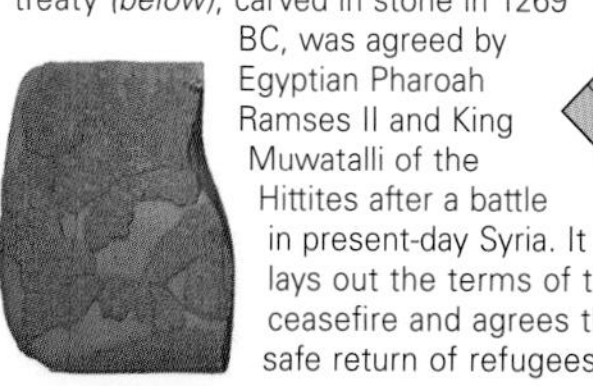

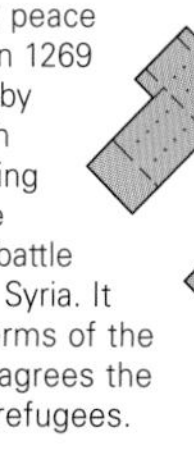

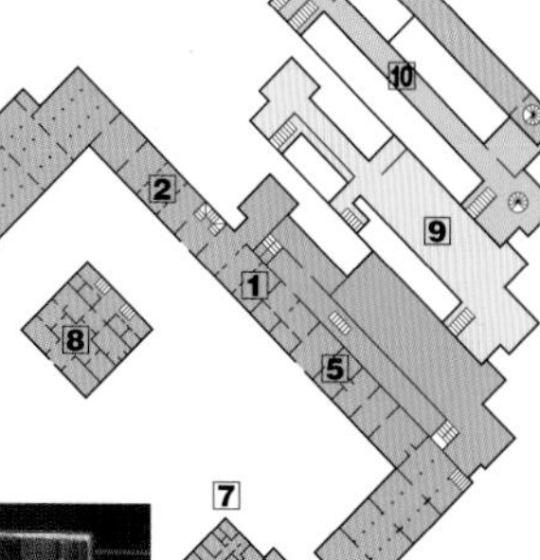

**Key**

- Third floor
- Second floor
- First floor
- Ground floor

## 7 Museum of the Ancient Orient

This section has well-preserved exhibits from Mesopotamia, Egypt and Babylon, including some of the world's first known writing – cuneiform clay tablets from 2700 BC.

## 8 Tiled Pavilion

Built in 1472 as a sports pavilion, this is the oldest secular building in Istanbul *(right)*. A masterpiece of İznik tiles itself, the pavilion also tells the story of Turkish ceramics, with displays from İznik and Kutahya.

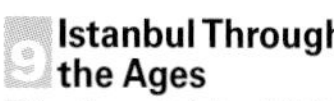

## 9 Istanbul Through the Ages

This thoughtful exhibit provides a fascinating insight into the city, with maps, plans and drawings alongside exhibits such as the 14th-century bell from the Galata Tower.

## 10 Anatolia and Troy Gallery

Thousands of years of history are imaginatively timelined in this long gallery. On one side you can travel through Anatolia from the Stone Age to the Iron Age. On the other wall, follow the history of Troy from 3000 BC to the 1st century AD.

### Ancient Welcome

Visitors are greeted by an eclectic assortment of archaeological artifacts. In the entrance hall to the main museum stands a statue of the Egyptian god Bes. At the foot of the stairs to the Museum of the Ancient Orient are two basalt lions from Samal, dating from the 8th century BC. Outside the main museum are porphyry sarchophagi, from the 4th–5th century AD, thought to be those of Byzantine emperors. The portico itself is modelled on the 4th-century-BC Sarcophagus of the Mourning Women.

*Also worth a visit are galleries devoted to Byzantium, Cyprus and Syria-Palestine. There's a children's museum in the new wing.*

# TOP 10 Grand Bazaar

*From the painted arches to the shopfronts gleaming with lanterns, piled with carpets or heaped with spices, the Kapalı Çarşı is a fantasy of Eastern opulence. Founded in 1461 by Sultan Mehmet II, the bazaar was designed as the trading heart of an empire. In addition to shops, banks, storerooms and cafés, it had travellers' accommodation, a bathhouse, mosques and a school. Destroyed several times by earthquake and fire, it has always bounced back. It offers a compelling and entertaining – if potentially expensive – day out.*

*Entrance to the Old Bazaar*

**The hotels, school and bathhouse that were once part of the bazaar have gone; now the market has a police station, ATM machines, public toilets and other necessities for keeping its droves of visitors happy.**

**There are small tea and coffee shops scattered throughout the market, as well as several good kebab shops, a couple of restaurants and a range of upmarket cafés.**

- *Map N3*
- *Open 8:30am–7pm Mon–Sat (surrounding street markets are usually open longer and on Sun)*
- *Free*
- *www.kapalicarsi.org.tr*

## Top 10 Features

1. İç Bedesten
2. Jewellers' Street
3. Carpet Sellers
4. Outdoor Stalls
5. Street Names
6. Fountains
7. Sandal Bedesten
8. Gates
9. Zincirli Han
10. Valide Han

### 1 İç Bedesten

This was the bazaar's first building, a Byzantine structure converted in 1461 into a sturdy lockup in which jewellery was traded and slaves were auctioned. Today it is used to sell precious goods such as antiques and rare icons.

### 2 Jewellers' Street (Kalpakçılar Başı Caddesi)

The bazaar's widest street runs along the southern edge of the market, its shop windows piled high with jewels and precious metals. Around 100,000 kg (220,460 lb) of gold is traded in the bazaar each year. Gold jewellery is sold by weight, with a little added for craftsmanship.

### 3 Carpet Sellers

The bazaar is home to Istanbul's finest carpet dealers, as well as lesser traders keen to sell you a hall runner or a bedside rug. Shops are scattered through out the market especially near the İç Bedesten on Halıcılar Çarşısı Caddesi.

For tips on shopping **See p42–3** For tips on carpets **See p44–5**

## 4 Outdoor Stalls

Surrounding the covered market is a maze of tiny lanes, with stalls selling carpets, souvenirs, clothes and vegetables. Locals shop here.

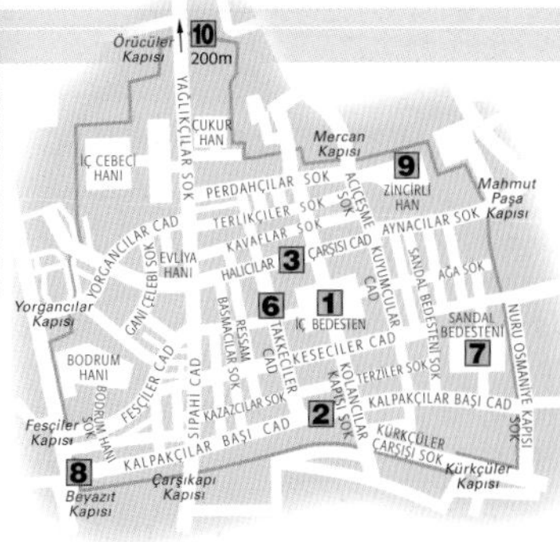


## 5 Street Names

At one time, each part of the bazaar had its own specialism, as indicated by the street names. Look for the *terlikçiler* (slipper-makers), *aynacılar* (mirror-makers), *fesçiler* (fez-makers), *yorgancılar* (quilt-makers), *kazazcılar* (silk-thread-makers) and *kürkçüler* (fur-makers).

## 6 Fountains

Two marble and copper fountains provided drinking water for the market traders before modern plumbing was installed. According to an 1880 survey, there were also 16 drinking-water posts, 1 fountain reservoir, and 8 wells for fire-fighters.

## 7 Sandal Bedesten

In the southeast corner of the bazaar, the 15th-century Sandal Bedesten, its roof of 20 brick domes propped up by pillars, is the former antiques market. It now hosts a carpet auction every Wednesday at 1pm.

## 8 Gates

Twenty-two gates lead into the covered bazaar from all directions. The Beyazıt Gate, rebuilt after an earthquake in 1894, is marked with the *tughra* (imperial sign) of Sultan Abdül Hamit II, and the happy assurance that "God loves tradesmen".

## 9 Zincirli Han

The *hans* provided accommodation, food and stables for travelling traders. This one, the oldest of 40 in the area, has been lovingly restored and is now occupied by Şişko Osman Halıcılık, a leading carpet dealer.

## 10 Valide Han

Constructed in 1651, this building (the largest caravanserai in Istanbul) has been sadly neglected. Today it contains a mix of residential, gallery and workshop space.

### Facts and Figures

The Grand Bazaar is one of the world's largest buildings, containing a network of 61 covered streets and enclosing an area of 307,000 sq m (3,305,000 sq ft). Every day in this teeming marketplace, as many as 30,000 traders in 4,500 shops befriend and haggle with up to 400,000 shoppers – both locals and visitors from all around the world. In business since its foundation in 1461, the bazaar is the world's oldest covered market.

*Taxis near the Grand Bazaar have a bad reputation; some drivers charge up to ten times the going rate* (see also p104).

# TOP 10 Süleymaniye Mosque

*One of the finest creations of the Ottoman Empire's greatest architect, Sinan, Süleymaniye Camii was built in 1550–57 for Süleyman I. He established this magnificent hilltop mosque as a charitable foundation* (külliye) *as well as a place of worship – and it stands in a vast complex that includes* medreses, *a* hamam, *a hospital and a caravanserai. The mosque's towering domes dominate the skyline in a matchless display of imperial power, while its delicate calligraphy, stained-glass windows and decorative carvings add a lightness of touch. Süleyman and his wife Roxelana are buried in tombs in the courtyard.*

*Exterior view of mosque*

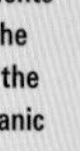

**Take a few moments after exploring the mosque to visit the University's Botanic Gardens, next door.**

**There are plenty of options for refreshment here, with the Darüzziyafe Restaurant** ***(see p71)*** **and Lalezar Café in the old soup kitchens, and a row of cafés right opposite the main entrance to the complex.**

- *Prof Siddik Sami Onar Cad*
- *Map M2*
- *(0212) 522 02 98*
- *Open 9am–7pm daily (closed at prayer times); Süleyman's tomb open 9:30am–4:30pm; Sinan's tomb open 9am–5pm Tue, Wed, Fri, Sun;* hamam *open 7am–midnight daily*
- *Free (adm charge for* hamam*).*

## Top 10 Features

1. Sinan's Tomb
2. Süleyman's Tomb
3. Mosque Interior
4. Courtyard
5. Medreses
6. Addicts' Alley
7. İmaret
8. Hamam
9. Caravanserai
10. Views

### 1 Sinan's Tomb

Sinan designed his own triangular mausoleum on the site of the house in which he lived while building the mosque, just beyond the northwest corner of the complex. It is a modest memorial to a prodigious talent.

### 2 Süleyman's Tomb

Sultan Süleyman I, "the Magnificent", lies in a grandiose and highly decorated garden tomb *(above)*, with an ebony, mother-of-pearl and ivory door and a dome inlaid with tiny ceramic stars.

### 3 Mosque Interior

The interior is simple and serene. The blue, white and gold dome *(above)* contains 200 stained-glass windows. The *mihrab* and pulpit are made from white marble decorated with İznik tiles.

### 4 Courtyard

This great courtyard *(above)* is surrounded by a colonnade of porphyry, Marmara and pink Egyptian columns, said to be recycled from the Hippodrome.

*After visiting the tomb of Süleyman, take a look at that of his wife, Roxelana – one of the most formidable women in Turkish history.*

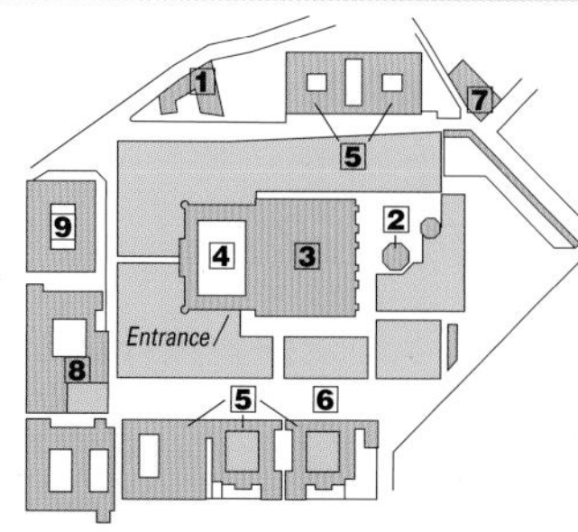


### 5 Medreses

Two of the six *medreses* (colleges) *(above)* – once part of the Imperial religious school providing theological and general education – house Süleyman's library of 110,000 manuscripts.

### 6 Addicts' Alley

The cafés of "Addicts' Alley" *(above)* – formally known as Prof Siddik Sami Onar Caddesi – once sold opium and hashish. It still has its cafés, but now the drug of choice is tobacco smoked in a water pipe *(nargile)*.

### 7 İmaret

The mosque kitchens not only fed the many workers, students, teachers and priests in the complex, but ran a soup kitchen for up to 1,000 people a day.

### 8 Hamam

This mosque's *hamam* is a mixed sex bathhouse, which makes it good for families. Somewhat alarmingly, it offers all visitors free life insurance during their bath!

### 9 Caravanserai

The mosque was a full-service complex – in the caravanserai, visitors and their animals could find food and lodging.

### 10 Views

The terraced gardens outside the main complex offer fine views *(below)* across the Golden Horn to the Galata Tower.

## Sinan

The incomparable Mimar Sinan, builder of 144 mosques and over 221 other buildings, never trained as an architect. He was born Greek Orthodox in 1489, and was conscripted to serve in the sultan's elite Janissary (New Army) Corps. He rose through the ranks to become Commander of the Infantry Cadet Corps, responsible for military engineering works, then in 1536 was appointed Architect of the Abode of Felicity by Süleyman. He held the post until his death aged 99 in 1588. Sinan considered the Selimiye Mosque in Edirne *(see p53)* his best work.

*Climb to the gallery in the mosque's northeast corner for some of the finest views of Istanbul available anywhere in the city.*

# TOP 10 Church of St Saviour in Chora

*The Church of St Saviour in Chora is home to one of the world's finest collections of Byzantine art: more than 100 magnificent mosaics and frescoes depicting biblical images. They were commissioned in 1315–21 by Byzantine statesman Theodore Metochites, who also restored the 11th-century church on the site. The church was converted into a mosque in 1511 and is known by locals as Kariye Mosque (Kariye Camii). Its works of art slipped into obscurity until they were rediscovered in 1860. Restoration began in 1948.*

*Exterior view*

**Photography is permitted, but flash is forbidden. Note that it is practically impossible to focus unless you use a tripod.**

**The Asitane Restaurant next door is a pleasant garden café, and one of the best places in Istanbul to eat traditional Ottoman cuisine.**

- *Kariye Camii Sok, Kariye Meydanı, Edirnekapı*
- *Map B2*
- *(0212) 631 92 41*
- *Open 9am–4:30pm (7pm in summer) Thu–Tue*
- *Adm 15 TL*

## Top 10 Features

1. Exterior
2. Genealogy of Christ
3. Anastasis Fresco
4. Parecclesion
5. Ministry of Christ
6. Mosaic of Theodore Metochites
7. The Last Judgment
8. Life of the Virgin
9. Infancy of Christ
10. Dormition of the Virgin

### 1 Exterior

Walk round the back of the church to experience the full impact of its architecture – with masonry of striped marble, six domes, layers of arches, undulating rooflines and, to one side, a minaret.

### 2 Genealogy of Christ

The two domes of the inner narthex (western entrance) portray 66 of Christ's forebears. In one dome *(above)*, Christ is surrounded by ancestors including Adam, Abraham, Jacob and Jacob's 12 sons. In the other, the Virgin and Child survey the kings of the House of David.

### 3 Anastasis Fresco

This resurrection fresco *(main image)* depicts Christ pulling Adam and Eve from their graves, while the gates of hell are broken and Satan lies bound at Christ's feet.

### 4 Parecclesion

A funerary chapel south of the main church, this is a glory of frescoes depicting judgment and resurrection *(below)*. The unmarked tomb in the north wall may be that of Theodore Metochites.

*There was an earlier (6th-century) church on this site, but nothing remains of it.*

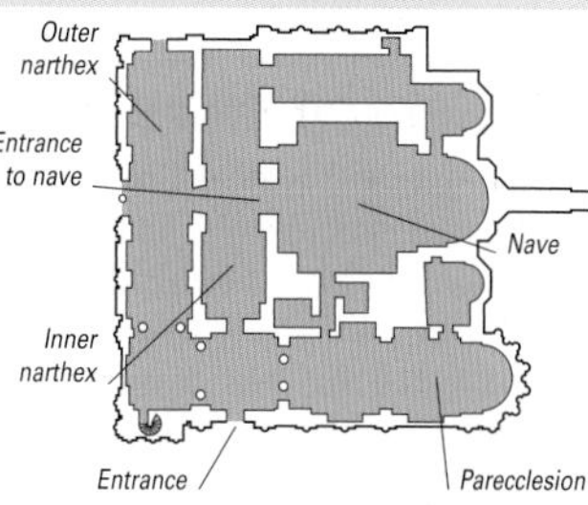


## 5 Ministry of Christ

The vaults of seven bays in the outer narthex and the south bay of the inner narthex detail the ministry of Christ *(above)*, including his temptation and miracles such as the wedding at Cana and the healing of the sick.

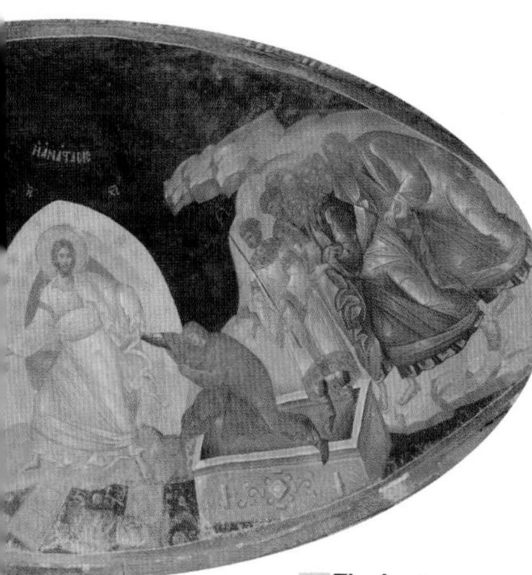

## 6 Mosaic of Theodore Metochites

Over the door leading from the inner narthex to the nave is a superb mosaic *(above)* depicting Theodore Metochites in a large turban presenting his church to Christ, who raises a hand in blessing.

## 7 The Last Judgment

In the main dome of the Paracclesion is a vision of the Last Judgment, with Christ in Majesty flanked by the Virgin Mary, John the Baptist and the Apostles. Adam and Eve kneel at Christ's feet.

## 8 Life of the Virgin

Twenty mosaics in the inner narthex depict the life of the Virgin Mary, based on the apocryphal 2nd-century Gospel of St James. They include images of Mary's first steps (at six months old), her time as a temple attendant (aged 3–13), and Joseph arriving home to find her pregnant.

## 9 Infancy of Christ

Scenes from Christ's infancy are depicted in the semicircular panels of the outer narthex. Based on New Testament accounts, they include the Journey to Bethlehem, Mary and Joseph enrolling for taxation, the Nativity, and the terrible Massacre of the Innocents.

## 10 Dormition of the Virgin

This beautiful mosaic in the nave *(above)* shows Christ sitting beside his mother's coffin, cradling a baby that represents her soul. Above is Ashrael, the Angel of Death.

### Layout

You now enter through a side door, but the main entrance was originally by way of a long porch, the outer narthex, which leads into an inner narthex. In the alcoves of these two porches you find the majority of the mosaics. The inner narthex opens into the main body of the church (the nave). At the far end, the altar stands in front of the semicircular apse, flanked by the Prothesis (Communion chapel) and Diakonikon (vestry). To one side is a separate funerary chapel, the Parecclesion.

*Like many other former places of worship in Istanbul, the Church of St Saviour in Chora is now a museum.*

# Top 10 Çemberlitaş Baths

*No stay in Istanbul would be complete without a bout of steaming, soaping, scrubbing and massaging in a Turkish bath* (hamam). *Çemberlitaş, built in 1584, is commonly hailed as one of the most beautiful. Designed by Sinan, it was commissioned by Selim II's wife Nur Banu as a way of providing financial support for the Atik Valide Sultan Mosque in Üsküdar* (see p95), *of which she was sponsor. Today Çemberlitaş is still used by Turks, but is most popular with tourists and photographers – it's a regular location for film and fashion shoots.*

A halvet *in the hot room*

**If you are planning to stay in the *hamam* for any length of time, take a small bottle of water in with you.**

**The baths are sited halfway between the Grand Bazaar and Sultanahmet Square, and are an easy walk from either. The surrounding area is bursting with cafés, tea shops and restaurants – take your pick.**

- *Vezir Hanı Cad 8*
- *Map P4*
- *(0212) 522 7974*
- *Open 6am–midnight daily*
- *Adm 45 TL (69 TL with massage, 117 TL with oil massage)*
- *www.cemberlitashamami.org*

## Top 10 Features

1. Entrance
2. Men's Section
3. Women's Section
4. Dressing Room
5. Hot Room
6. Private Cubicles
7. Navel Stone
8. Cool Room
9. Oil Massage Room
10. Extras

### 1 Entrance

At the ticket office, you are given a *pestemal* (a sarong-like garment, for modesty), a *kese* (a coarse mitt for scrubbing the body down) and tokens to give to the attendants. Men and women are then sent off to separate sections.

### 2 Men's Section

Originally the *hamam* consisted of two identical suites of rooms, each with a separate entrance. The men's section of the baths is still exactly as envisaged by its creator, Sinan.

### 3 Women's Section

The women's changing area was lost in 1868, when Divanyolu Caddesi was widened, so women now change in a corridor; but their hot room is unaltered.

### 4 Dressing Room (Camekan)

Here *(below)*, an attendant will assign you a locker and give you a pair of slippers. Most people go nude under the *pestemal*, but wear a swimsuit if you wish to.

*Today, most baths operate separate hours for men and women. In Ottoman times, a breach of segregation was a capital offence.*

## 5 Hot Room (Sıcaklık)

The hot room *(main image)* has a domed ceiling supported by 12 arches that rise from marble columns. The dome is pitted with glass "elephants' eyes", which channel the light through the steam to polka-dot the floor.

## 6 Private Cubicles (Halvets)

Around the walls are a number of private cubicles with taps running cold, warm and hot water, which you can use to wash or cool down if the heat gets too much for you.

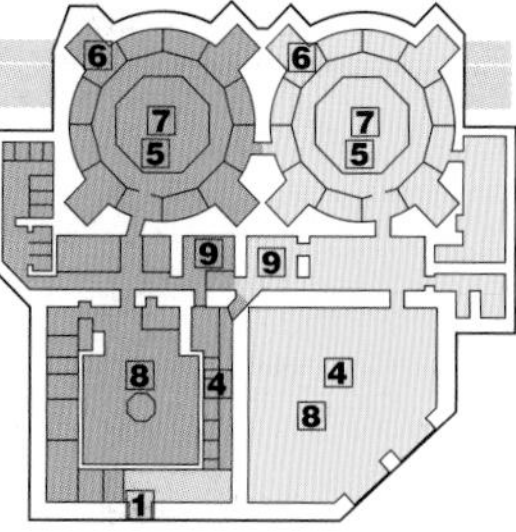


**Key**

Men's Section

Women's Section

## 7 Navel Stone (Göbek Taşı)

In the centre of the hot room is a large slab of marble *(left)*. Lie down and wait for the attendant. You will be covered in soap suds, and scrubbed all over with the *kese*. Then you will be lathered again, washed with a cloth, and soap-massaged *(below)*. Finally, your hair will be washed, and you will be vigorously rinsed with buckets of water.

## 8 Cool Room (Soğukluk)

The cool room *(left)* is the place to sit and chat. The men's is as elegant as it was in Sinan's day; the women's a little less welcoming. Afterwards, head back to change, or go for your oil massage.

## 9 Oil Massage Room

You will be one of several people being massaged *(right)* on a row of beds under bright lights. It's worth any discomfort you may experience – you'll feel great after.

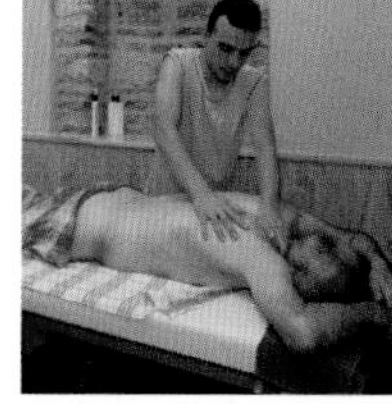

## 10 Extras

Take as much time as you like to return to the steam room or sit in the cool room. If you want the full works, the attendants will be happy to give you a manicure, pedicure or facial.

### Ancient Customs

The direct descendant of the Graeco-Roman bath, the *hamam* was eagerly adopted by Islamic invaders who really did believe that cleanliness is next to Godliness; the bath was a chance not only to cleanse the skin and detoxify the body, but also to restore the spirit. For women, time in the *hamam* was a welcome escape from the narrow world in which they spent their lives, as well as a place to check out potential daughters-in-law.

*It is customary to tip the attendants around 10 per cent.*

# TOP 10 Dolmabahçe Palace

*In 1843, Sultan Abdül Mecit, who wanted to reinvent the Ottoman Empire in a European image, employed Armenian architects Karabet and Nikoğos Balyan to build a luxurious new palace on the Bosphorus shore. Dolmabahçe Sarayı, completed in 1856, is the result. Luxurious it certainly is, with 46 reception rooms and galleries, and lavish decoration in gold and crystal that rivals the Palace of Versailles in France. Ironically, this extravagance hastened the end of the Empire, and the last emperor fled from here into exile in 1922.*

*The Swan Fountain in the Imperial Gardens*

**Admission to the palace is by guided tour only. There are two itineraries: one of the Selamlık (the areas reserved for men, including the Ceremonial Hall); the other of the Harem (including the living quarters of the royal women, the sultan's private quarters, and Atatürk's bedroom, bathroom and study).**

**There is a café in the Clock Tower, and toilets near both entrances.**

- *Dolmabahçe Cad*
- *Map C5* • *(0212) 236 90 00* • *Tram: Kabataş, then a 5-minute walk*
- *Open 9am–4pm Tue, Wed, Fri–Sun (to 3pm, Oct–Feb)* • *Adm 30 TL for Selamlık, 20 TL for Harem, 40 TL for a combined ticket*
- *www.dolmabahce.gov.tr*

## Top 10 Features

1. Gates
2. Waterfront Façade
3. Ceremonial Hall
4. Harem
5. State Rooms
6. Atatürk's Rooms
7. Crystal Staircase
8. Sultan's Bathrooms
9. Clock Tower
10. Gardens

### 1 Gates

The palace had two ceremonial entrances, both highly ornamented: the Treasury Gate, which is now the main entrance, and the Imperial Gate *(above)*. Both gates still have a guard of honour.

### 2 Waterfront Façade

The marble façade *(below)* is 284 m (930 ft) long. The State Rooms are on the left, the Ceremonial Hall in the centre, and the Harem on the right.

### 3 Ceremonial Hall (Muayede Salonu)

The dome in this vast hall *(above)* is 36 m (118 ft) high. The crystal chandelier, a gift from Queen Victoria of England, has 750 lights and weighs 4.5 tonnes (more than 9,000 lb). It is the world's largest chandelier.

*If you only have time for one of the two tours, visit the Selamlık: the Ceremonial Hall and Crystal Staircase are unmissable.*

## 4 Harem

A fascinating mix of East and West, the Harem has several apartments, furnished to various grades of luxury (for the sultan, his mother, wives, concubines, servants and guests) – also baths, a school, a maternity ward and a central salon *(left)* where the wives and concubines would meet for tea, chat and embroidery.

## 5 State Rooms (Selamlık)

The rooms on the palace's seaward side were used by the Grand Vizier and ministers, while those on the landward side were administrative offices. They are all lavishly decorated and furnished.

## 7 Crystal Staircase

This ornate double-horseshoe staircase has balusters of Baccarat crystal. It links the administrative offices with the ceremonial and function rooms upstairs.

## 6 Atatürk's Rooms

In the first years of the republic, Atatürk used the palace as his Istanbul base, keeping an office and bedroom *(above)* in the Harem. He died here, from cirrhosis of the liver, on 10 November 1938 – all the palace's clocks are set to 9:05am, the moment of his death.

### Atatürk

Born in 1881, Mustafa Kemal Paşa rose to prominence in 1915, leading Turkish forces to victory at Gallipoli. A leader of the Young Turks republican movement, he seized his moment following the end of World War I, abolishing the sultanate in 1922 and declaring a republic in 1923. As Turkey's first president, he Westernized the country – introducing the Latin alphabet, compulsory schooling, and rights for women. He is still idolized as the "Father of the Turks" (Atatürk); it is illegal in Turkey to criticize him publicly.

## 8 Sultan's Bathrooms

The Sultan had two bathrooms: one in the main palace, faced in marble; the other in the Harem, decorated in violet flowers and with a Murano glass mirror.

## 9 Clock Tower

The four-storey tower, 27 m (90 ft) high, was added to the palace in 1890, during the reign of Sultan Abdül Hamit II *(see p89)*. The clock – which still keeps time – was built by the celebrated Parisian clockmaker Paul Garnier.

## 10 Gardens

The palace and gardens stand on reclaimed land (the name Dolmabahçe means "Filled Garden"). In addition to the palace and its 16 external pavilions, the grounds once held a flour mill, pharmacy, aviary, glass factory and foundry.

*The former Crown Prince Pavilion, adjacent to Dolmabahçe Palace, now houses the Museum of Painting and Sculpture* (see p92).

# TOP 10 Bosphorus Cruise

*The Istanbul skyline is justifiably one of the most famous cityscapes in the world, and while there are many places from which to admire it, by far the best is the deck of a boat on the Bosphorus. After the bustle of the city centre, a trip up the Bosphorus gives you an entirely different perspective on the city. Give your lungs a break from breathing in traffic fumes and your feet a rest from trudging pavements. Take the local ferry for a modest fare, and spend a day floating serenely along the straits past magnificent shores and wooden villas.*

*Bosphorus Bridge*

**The ferry journey to Rumeli Hisarı takes around 1 hour 45 minutes then goes straight back. There are only short stops en route, so take the local bus back if you'd like to visit any of the sights along the river (but be warned, it is slow).**

**Food is available on the ferry and there are various food facilities at the last stop on Anadolu Kavaği.**

- *Departs from Eminönü Boğaz Hattı Pier*
- *Map F4*
- *(0212) 444 18 51*
- *Departures daily, Apr–Nov: 1:35pm, Dec–Mar: 10:35am*
- *Fare 10 TL short circle cruise, 25 TL round trip (the full Bosphorus cruise)*
- *www.sehirhatlari.com.tr*

### Top 10 Features

1. Eminönü Pier
2. Leander's Tower
3. Dolmabahçe Palace
4. Ortaköy
5. Bosphorus Bridge
6. Beylerbeyi Palace
7. Arnavutköy and Bebek
8. Fortress of Europe
9. Sarıyer
10. Anadolu Kavağı

### 1 Eminönü Pier

The Bosphorus ferry departs from Eminönü port *(main picture)*, the city's busiest ferry terminal. Pick up a pretzel or fish sandwich from a street vendor.

### 2 Leander's Tower (Kız Kulesi)

This tower on an island offshore from Üsküdar is a restaurant. Its Turkish name means "Maiden's Tower", after a legendary princess kept there; the English name refers to a hero of Greek myth *(see p95)*.

### 3 Dolmabahçe Palace (Dolmabahçe Sarayı)

Sultan Abdül Mecit virtually mortgaged the Ottoman Empire to build this lavish palace *(above)* in the 1850s.

### 4 Ortaköy

One of the prettiest villages on the straits, at the foot of the Bosphorus Bridge, Ortaköy *(above)* is a weekend retreat for İstanbullus.

### 5 Bosphorus Bridge (Boğaziçi Köprüsü)

Completed in 1973, this 1,560-m (5,120-ft) long bridge, stretching between Ortaköy and Beylerbeyi, was the first to link Europe and Asia.


*For more on the Dolmabahçe Palace* **See pp26–7**

## 6 Beylerbeyi Palace (Beylerbeyi Sarayı) (Asian Side)

This delightfully fussy palace *(above)* was built as a summer annexe to the Dolmabahçe. It had no kitchens, and food was rowed across as required.

## 7 Arnavutköy and Bebek

The 19th-century wooden villas *(yalis)* that prettily line the waterfront along this central stretch of the Bosphorus are the city's most desirable real estate.

## 8 Fortress of Europe (Rumeli Hisarı)

This castle *(above)* was built by Mehmet the Conqueror in 1452 prior to his attack on Constantinople. Across the water stands the Fortress of Asia (Anadolu Hisarı), built in the late 14th century.

## 9 Sarıyer

This village *(right)* is the main fishing port on the Bosphorus. It has a historic fish market, as well as several good fish restaurants (with lovely views) near the shore.

## 10 Anadolu Kavağı (Asian Side)

This is the last stop for the ferry, and the locals make a good living selling fish lunches and ice cream to the tourists. There is a wonderful view from a 14th-century fort, the Genoese Castle, on the hill above *(left)*.

### It's All a Myth

When Greek goddess Hera sent a swarm of gnats to plague the beautiful Io, her rival for the affections of the god Zeus, Io turned herself into a cow and swam across the straits to escape, giving the Bosphorus its name – the "Ford of the Cow". In another Greek myth, Jason and the Argonauts rowed up the Bosphorus in search of the Golden Fleece – perhaps an echo of the Black Sea tradition of using a lamb's fleece to trap the gold when panning.

*For more on the Bosphorus and environs* **See pp88–93**

الله
جل جلاله

Left **Florence Nightingale in Selimiye Barracks** Right **Atatürk reviews his troops**

# Top 10 Moments in History

### 1 AD 330–95: Division of the Roman Empire

In 330, Constantine moved the capital of the Empire from Rome to the former Greek colony of Byzantium. It was initially called New Rome but later became Constantinople ("City of Constantine"). In 395, Theodosius divided the Empire between his sons, with the western half run from Rome and the eastern (Byzantine) half centred on Constantinople.

**Bust of Constantine**

### 2 1071: Battle of Manzikert

The Seljuk Turks from Persia defeated Byzantine forces at Manzikert and seized most of Anatolia. The Byzantines never recovered their eastern lands.

### 3 1204: Sack and Capture of Constantinople

The armies of the Fourth Crusade sacked Constantinople, driving the emperor into exile. Crusader rulers governed in Constantinople until 1261, when Byzantine Emperor Michael VIII Palaeologus recaptured the city.

**The Capture of Constantinople in 1204**

### 4 1453: Birth of Istanbul

Following years of Ottoman encroachment into the Byzantine Empire, Sultan Mehmet II captured Constantinople, renaming it İslambol ("the City of Islam"). The last Byzantine emperor, Constantine IX, died fighting on the city walls.

### 5 1529: Siege of Vienna

The Ottoman Empire reached its maximum extent under Süleyman I. In 1526, he had taken control of southern Hungary. In the spring of 1529, he mustered a huge military force with the aim of consolidating his Hungarian gains and moving on to Vienna. A combination of serious flooding en route and a spirited defence led by a German mercenary, Niklas Graf Salm, sent the Turks packing and marked the end of Ottoman expansion in Western Europe.

### 6 1777: Turkish Delight

Ali Muhiddin Hacı Bekir, confectioner to the imperial court, invented a chewy sweet flavoured with rosewater and coated in icing sugar: *lokum* ("morsel of contentment"), better known as Turkish delight.

Preceding pages **Interior view of Haghia Sophia**

7 **1853–6: Crimean War** When Russia began to encroach on Ottoman territory, Britain and France weighed in on the side of the Turks. Florence Nightingale set up a hospital in Istanbul, defining modern nursing practice *(see p96)*.

8 **1919–23: Birth of the Republic** Mustafa Kemal Paşa – or Atatürk ("Father of the Turks") – led a bloodless revolution that abolished the sultanate, and fought a fierce war of independence. In 1923, as first president of the new Republic of Turkey, he moved the capital to Ankara, leaving Istanbul without political status for the first time in 1,600 years.

**Construction of the Bosphorus Bridge, 1972**

9 **1973: Bosphorus Bridge** The Bosphorus Bridge was opened between Ortaköy and Beylerbeyi, linking European Turkey to Asian Anatolia.

10 **2010: Istanbul European Capital of Culture** The city was chosen to be one of 2010's European Capitals of Culture. A programme of events showcased Istanbul's historic and traditional cultural heritage.

## Top 10 Notable Ottoman Emperors

1 **Osman Gazi (1299–1326)** The Ottoman dynasty takes its name from that of its founder, Osman. In 1301, his forces won the first Ottoman victory against the Byzantine Empire at the Battle of Baphaeon.

2 **Orhan Gazi (1326–59)** Orhan moved the Ottoman capital to Bursa and established Islam as the state religion.

3 **Murat I (1359–89)** Murat founded the Janissary Corps, an elite group within the Ottoman army.

4 **Beyazıt I (1389–1402)** Beyazıt began the Muslim colonization of Serbia.

5 **Mehmet II the Conqueror (1451–81)** In 1453, Mehmet captured Constantinople from its Byzantine rulers. He laid out a new city on the rubble, and founded Topkapı Palace.

6 **Süleyman I the Magnificent (1520–66)** A conqueror, lawmaker and patron of the arts, Süleyman presided over the golden age of Ottoman rule *(see p58)*.

7 **Mehmet III (1595–1603)** Mehmet's mother had 18 of his 19 brothers strangled so that he could take the throne.

8 **Osman II (1618–22)** The Janissaries raped and strangled Osman at Yedikule after his failed attempt to curb their power.

9 **Mahmut II (1808–39)** Mahmut wiped out the Janissary Corps, slaughtering thousands in the purge.

10 **Mehmet VI (1918–22)** The last of the Ottoman emperors fled into European exile in November 1922.

*The name İstanbul was in use from the 10th century onwards. It derives from the Greek "eis ten polin" (literally, "in the city").*

Left **Museum of Turkish and Islamic Arts** Centre **Rahmi Koç Museum** Right **Archaeological Museum**

# Top 10 Museums and Galleries

### 1 Topkapı Palace (Topkapı Sarayı)

The buildings are spectacular, some of the collections are even more so – from the sea of Chinese porcelain in the kitchens to the Treasury, with its ostentatious display of jewellery, carved ivory and great rocks of emerald. Religious treasures include hair from the Prophet's beard *(see pp8–11)*.

### 2 Archaeological Museum (Arkeoloji Müzesi)

Don't miss the late-4th-century-AD marble tomb of Abdalonymus of Sidon, known as the "Alexander Sarcophagus". Its high-relief carving depicts Alexander the Great defeating the Persians at the Battle of Issus in 333 BC *(see pp16–17)*.

### 3 Military Museum (Askeri Müze)

Among the many fascinating exhibits are curved daggers *(cembiyes)* carried by 15th-century Ottoman footsoldiers, and the vast imperial tents used by sultans on campaign. The Mehter Band, founded in the 14th century, plays Ottoman military music daily at 3pm *(see p80)*.

### 4 Sakıp Sabancı Museum (Sakıp Sabancı Müzesi)

Known locally as the "Horse Mansion", this lovely museum houses the collection of the late Turkish business tycoon Sakıp Sabancı, encompassing 500 years of Ottoman calligraphy, and Ottoman and Turkish painting of the 19th and 20th centuries. The museum also hosts touring art exhibitions *(see p91)*.

**Horse sculpture in the grounds of the Sakıp Sabancı Museum**

### 5 Museum of Turkish and Islamic Arts (Türk ve İslam Eserleri Müzesi)

This wonderful collection, in the 16th-century palace of İbrahim Paşa, spans 1,300 years of the finest works of Turkish and Islamic art, including beautiful calligraphy, manuscripts and Turkish miniatures *(see p57)*.

**Mehter Band at the Military Museum**

## 6 Istanbul Museum of Modern Art (İstanbul Modern Sanat Müzesi)

For centuries, Turkish art has been known for tradition rather than innovation, but contemporary Turkish artists are exploring new avenues. Set in a beautifully converted warehouse on the Bosphorus, the Istanbul Modern is an ideal platform *(see p89)*.

## 7 Rahmi Koç Museum (Rahmi Koç Müzesi)

An Ottoman foundry and nearby shipyard on the Golden Horn are the perfect setting for this world-class collection of all things mechanical, from vintage cars to model planes – and even a submarine *(see p74)*.

## 8 Sadberk Hanım Museum (Sadberk Hanım Müzesi)

Two lovingly restored Bosphorus mansions house an inspiring collection of ancient Anatolian artifacts, Ottoman costumes and ceramics *(see p91)*.

**Attic vase, Sadberk Hanım Museum**

## 9 Naval Museum (Deniz Müzesi)

For centuries, the Ottoman navy ruled the seas, and its achievements are celebrated in this marvellous museum. Among the highlights are flamboyantly decorated royal barges *(see p89)*.

## 10 Pera Museum (Pera Müzesi)

The Pera is a museum with an intriguing mix of fine art, modern exhibitions and ancient weights and measures *(see p80)*.

## Top 10 Less-Famous Museums

**1 santralistanbul**
See contemporary art in the old Silahtarağa power plant. *Eyüp • (0212) 311 78 78*

**2 Mevlevi Monastery**
Whirling dervishes are the main draw in this monastery-turned-museum *(see p82)*.

**3 Yapı Kredi Vedat Nedim Tör Museum**
The Yapı Kredi bank funds this small private collection of art and artifacts *(see p82)*.

**4 Railway Museum, Sirkeci Station**
The Orient Express silver service is the star among 300 exhibits *(see p58)*.

**5 SAV Automobile Museum**
Inspect the pick of a century of motor transport, from Rolls Royce to Ferrari *(see p92)*.

**6 Aşiyan Museum**
A Bosphorus mansion pays homage to 20th-century poets and thinkers *(see p90)*.

**7 Bilim ve Teknoloji Müzesi**
See displays of historical tools from astronomy and medicine, to war. *Has Ahirlar Binası, Gülhane Parkı • (0212) 528 80 65*

**8 Florence Nightingale Museum**
The museum includes the nurse's private quarters and surgery room *(see p96)*.

**9 Aviation Museum (Havacılık Müzesi)**
This collection of old planes and models is near Atatürk International airport. *Yeşilköy • (0212) 663 24 90*

**10 Atatürk Museum**
This suburban house is now a memorial museum to the great man. *Halaskargazi Cad, Şişli • Map T4 • (0212) 240 63 19*

Left **Haghia Sophia** Centre **Church of St Saviour in Chora** Right **A gate in the Theodosian Walls**

# TOP 10 Byzantine Monuments

### 1 Haghia Sophia (Ayasofya)

Built by Emperor Justinian in the 6th century, Haghia Sophia is one of the world's greatest architectural achievements. Justinian was so proud of his basilica that he proclaimed: "Glory to God who has thought me worthy to finish this work. Solomon, I have outdone you" *(see pp12–13)*.

### 2 Hippodrome (At Meydanı)

Once a Byzantine race track 450 m (1500 ft) long, the Hippodrome could hold 100,000 people. It was the scene of celebrations and, on occasion, bloodshed; the Nika Riots in 532 ended with 30,000 dead *(see p57)*.

**Relief carved on base of Eqyptian Obelisk, Hippodrome**

### 3 Cisterns

To ensure good water supply in times both of peace and of siege, the Byzantines built a series of vast underground water cisterns beneath their city. The finest are the Basilica Cistern (Yerebatan Sarnıcı) *(see p58)* and the Cistern of 1,001 Columns (Binbirdirek Sarnıcı) *(see p60)*.

**Basilica Cistern**

### 4 Church of St Saviour in Chora (Kariye Camii)

The main reason to visit this 11th-century Byzantine church is its glorious collection of mosaics and frescoes, which depict biblical scenes *(see pp22–3)*.

### 5 Theodosian Walls (Teodos II Surları)

Over the course of 1,000 years, the curtain walls built by Emperor Theodosius II in 412–22 proved to be a necessity – they withstood more than 20 attacks by Huns, Arabs, Bulgarians, Turks and Russians, finally succumbing to the Ottomans in 1453 (see p32). The walls have now been partially restored *(see p75)*.

### 6 Mosaics Museum (Mozaik Müzesi)

Only fragments remain of the Great Palace of the Byzantine Emperors. This small museum houses one of them – the mosaic passageway, discovered in the 1930s, that led from the palace to the royal box in the Hippodrome. The beautifully crafted floor depicts wild animals and hunting scenes *(see p60)*.

### 7 Bucoleon Palace (Bukoleon Sarayı)

At the bottom of the hill behind Sultanahmet, built into the old sea wall, is the last standing fragment of the Imperial Bucoleon Palace *(see p61)*.

### 8 Aqueduct of Valens (Bozdoğan Kemeri)

This beautifully preserved 4th-century aqueduct, which remained in use until the 19th century, was a key part of the system that carried fresh water into the Byzantine capital from the Belgrade Forest *(see p73)*.

**Haghia Eirene**

### 9 Haghia Eirene (Aya İrini Kilisesi)

One of the oldest churches in the city, Haghia Eirene stands in the outer courtyard of the Topkapı Palace. It was the city's main church until Haghia Sophia was built. The church has excellent acoustics and is only open to the public for concerts *(see p61)*.

### 10 Church of the Pammakaristos (Fethiye Camii)

This large 12th-century Byzantine church served as the worldwide headquarters of the Greek Orthodox faith during the 15th and 16th centuries. It was converted to a mosque by Murat III in 1591. The former side chapel is now a museum housing some magnificent mosaics *(see p73)*.

## Top 10 Notable Byzantine Rulers

1. **Constantine (306–37)** Constantine moved the capital of the Roman Empire to Constantinople *(see p32)*.
2. **Theodosius II (408–50)** Theodosius codified the law, founded a university and built the city walls *(see p75)*.
3. **Justinian I (527–65)** Justinian founded many great buildings including Haghia Sophia *(see p12–13)*, as well as reforming the law.
4. **Theodora (527–48)** A bear-keeper's daughter turned stripper and prostitute, Theodora ruled alongside her husband Justinian I.
5. **Justinian II (685–95 and 705–11)** Justinian's enemies deposed him then cut off his nose, because a disfigured man could not be emperor. He later regained the throne wearing, it is said, a prosthetic nose of solid gold.
6. **Irene of Athens (797–802)** Irene was the first woman to rule the Empire on her own.
7. **Basil I (867–86)** The homosexual lover of Michael III, Basil was crowned joint emperor in 866, then killed Michael to rule alone.
8. **Zoë (1028–50)** Zoë wed three times after becoming empress aged 50.
9. **Romanus IV Diogenes (1067–71)** Romanus was defeated by the Seljuks at Manzikert in 1071 and was exiled as a result.
10. **Constantine XI Palaeologus (1449–53)** The last of the Byzantines died fighting on the city walls during the conquest of 1453.

eft **Atik Valide Mosque** Centre **Sinan's tomb, Süleymaniye Mosque** Right **Church of St George**



# TOP 10 Places of Worship

### 1 Süleymaniye Mosque (Süleymaniye Camii)

This vast mosque, which dominates the skyline of the Golden Horn, is the crowning achievement of Koca Mimar Sinan, greatest of Imperial architects *(see pp20–21)*. Built in 1550–57 in the grounds of the old palace, Eski Saray, it is a suitably grand memorial to its founder, Süleyman I *(see pp32, 33, 58)*.

**Blue Mosque**

### 2 Blue Mosque (Sultanahmet Camii)

Commissioned by Ahmet I, the Blue Mosque was built by the Imperial architect Mehmet Ağa, a pupil of the great Sinan, in 1609–16. It takes its name from the blue İznik tiles on its inner walls *(see pp14–15)*.

**The light and airy interior of Fatih Mosque**

### 3 Fatih Mosque (Fatih Camii)

The original Fatih Mosque was built by Mehmet II to celebrate his capture of Constantinople in 1453; its name means "the Conqueror's mosque". The present mosque was built in the 18th century, after an earthquake of 1766 destroyed the original *(see p73)*.

### 4 Eyüp Mosque (Eyüp Camii)

Also rebuilt after the 1766 earthquake, this mosque at the top of the Golden Horn is one of the holiest places in Islam. It is built around the tomb of a 7th-century saint, Eyüp el-Ensari, standard-bearer of the Prophet Mohammed *(see p74)*.

### 5 Atik Valide Mosque (Atik Valide Camii)

One of Istanbul's finest mosques and Sinan's last great work, the "Old Mosque of the Sultan's Mother" was completed in 1583 for the formidable Nur Banu, wife of Selim III and mother of Murat III *(see p95)*.

### 6 Church of St George (Aya Yorgi)

The Church of St George stands within the Greek Orthodox Patriarchate complex. Built in 1720, it includes a superb 11th-century mosaic of the Virgin Mary *(see p76)*.

*It is essential to dress modestly when visiting a mosque. It's also a good idea to wear shoes you can slip on and off easily.*

## 7 Neve Shalom Synagogue (Neve Şalom Sinagogu)

Built in 1949–51 for the Sephardic Jewish community, this is the largest of several synagogues in Istanbul. There have been Jews in the city since Roman times, but numbers rose in 1492 when Jews expelled from Spain were welcomed by the Ottomans. *Büyük Hendek Cad 67 • Map F2 • (0212) 293 75 66, 292 03 86 • Phone to visit*

## 8 Church of St Mary of the Mongols (Kanlı Kilise)

Princess Maria, illegitimate daughter of Byzantine Emperor Michael VIII Palaeologos, married Khan Abaka of the Mongols. On his death in 1281, she founded a convent and this church – Istanbul's only Greek Orthodox church to have been granted immunity from conversion to a mosque by Mehmet the Conqueror *(see p76)*.

**Detail, Church of St Mary of the Mongols**

## 9 Church of St Anthony of Padua (Sent Antuan Kilisesi)

Istanbul's largest Roman Catholic church, built in 1906–12, is also home to a small community of Franciscan monks *(see p82)*.

## 10 Christ Church

Consecrated in 1868 as the Crimean Memorial Church, this fine Gothic Revival building was renovated and renamed in the 1990s. It is the largest Protestant church in Istanbul *(see p82)*.

## Top 10 Tips on Islamic Etiquette

### 1 Shoes
Remove your shoes before entering a mosque or a Turkish home.

### 2 Men and Women
A man should not touch a woman (other than family), even to shake hands, unless the woman proffers her hand or cheek first.

### 3 Left Hand
In some Islamic countries one should avoid eating or passing food with the left hand; in Turkey this is not observed.

### 4 Pork and Alcohol
Although many people in Turkey do drink alcohol, you should never offer alcohol or pork to a Muslim – and do not consume yourself if unsure of your companions' views.

### 5 Family Rooms
Some restaurants and cafés have separate family rooms *(aile salonu)* into which women will automatically be conducted. Men may only sit there with their families.

### 6 Dress
Dress modestly – no bare knees, shoulders or midriffs (for either sex).

### 7 Covering the Head
It is considered polite for a woman to cover her head when entering a mosque.

### 8 Ramazan
Avoid eating and drinking in public during daylight hours in the month-long fast of Ramazan.

### 9 Sightseeing
Don't go sightseeing in mosques at prayer times (particularly noon on Fridays).

### 10 Joking about Islam
Don't joke about Islam or criticize anything related to it.

*There are around 20,000 Jews living in Istanbul today.*

Left **Fresh fish sandwiches** Centre **Cold *meze*, including *tarama* and *haydari*** Right ***İmam bayıldı***

# TOP 10 Culinary Highlights

### 1 Meze

Most Turkish meals begin with *meze* – collections of small starters. The range of *meze* is vast, and you can easily eat enough for a whole meal. Cold options range from *haydari* (yoghurt with mint and garlic) to *midye pilakisi* (mussels cooked in olive oil) or *çerkez tavuğu* (cold chicken in walnut and bread sauce). Hot options may include chicken liver kebabs, calamari, grilled cheese, or something more adventurous such as *koç yumurtası* (fried sheep's testicles).

### 2 İmam Bayıldı ("The Imam Fainted")

This strangely named dish of aubergine stuffed with tomatoes and onions is a Turkish classic – the Imam in question supposedly found it so delicious that he passed out in ecstasy. Aubergine is a fundamental ingredient of Turkish cuisine; it is said that Ottoman court chefs could prepare it in 150 ways.

### 3 Çoban Salatası ("Shepherd's Salad")

This salad combines tomato, cucumber, chopped pepper, lettuce, coriander, celery, lemon juice and olive oil in a light, healthy, colourful and refreshing dish. Turkish tomatoes are among the finest in the world.

### 4 Dolma

The word *dolma* means "filled up", and is used to describe any stuffed food, from walnuts to peppers or aubergine. The most common version, eaten cold, is vine leaves stuffed with rice, onion, nuts and herbs.

### 5 Kebabs and Köfte

Turkey's most famous culinary export is the kebab – called *kebap* in Turkish. *Döner kebap* is wafer-thin slices of roast meat (usually lamb) carved from a spit; the *şiş kebap* is cubed lamb or chicken grilled on a skewer. *Köfte* is minced meat cooked as meatballs or flattened onto a skewer and grilled as an *izgara kebap.*

**Kebabs and Köfte**

### 6 Seafood

Istanbul's proximity to the sea means that *taze balık* (fresh fish) is very popular with locals. The catch of the day is often grilled and served with rice or chips and salad. Shellfish and calamari are served as *meze*. A delicious Black Sea dish is *hamsi pilavı* (fresh anchovies and rice).

### 7 Stews (Güveç)

Often served in traditional *lokanta* restaurants *(see p110)* and generally popular in winter, hearty stews are mostly made with lamb, tomatoes and onions.

Döner kebap *translates literally as "rotating meat".*

8 **Börek**
These savoury pastries are served either as part of a *meze* or on their own as fast food. They can be flat or rolled, and are filled with cheese and onion, spinach or meat. They make an excellent light snack.

9 **Pastries**
Sweet pastries are sold in dedicated shops and by street vendors; tourist restaurants will offer them as dessert. The most famous is *baklava* (flaky pastry drenched in syrup), but there are many variations with honey, syrups, marzipan, almonds and pistachios. All are heaven to eat and calorie hell.

**Turkish pastries**

10 **Tea and Coffee**
The lifeblood of Turkey, both *çay* (tea) and *kahve* (coffee) are drunk black, strong and sweet, in small quantities. Tea is served all day and on all occasions. You can ask for it weaker and without sugar. Coffee is drunk less frequently; it is more expensive than tea, and is served with a glass of water. All instant coffee is known as Nescafé.

## Top 10 Culinary Specialities

1 **Elastic Ice Cream**
*Sahlepli dondurma* uses wild orchid tubers as a thickening agent. The ice cream can stretch into a "rope" 60 cm (2 ft) long!

2 **İşkembe Çorbası (Tripe Soup)**
This local delicacy is said to be good for hangovers.

3 **Kanlıca Yoghurt**
Firm and creamy, the yoghurt from Kanlıca is the country's finest.

4 **Lokum (Turkish Delight)**
Turkish Delight was invented by an Istanbul sweetmaker *(see p32)*. It's now sold everywhere and in many flavours, including mint and lemon. The original shop is still open. *Hamidiye Cad 81, Bahçekapı • Map Q2 • (0212) 522 85 43*

5 **Simit**
*Simit* is a round sesame bread like a New York pretzel.

6 **Gözleme**
*Gözleme* are large rolled pancakes with savoury stuffing.

7 **Mantı**
These pasta cushions are stuffed with minced lamb and served in a thin garlic sauce.

8 **Aşure (Noah's Pudding)**
As the story goes, this celebratory pudding was first made by Mrs Noah, from whatever scraps remained on the Ark at the end of the Flood.

9 **Elma Çayı (Apple Tea)**
You may be offered this as an alternative to tea when visiting carpet shops.

10 **Rakı**
A clear spirit, *rakı* can be made of any fruit, but most common is the aniseed-based version similar to Greek *ouzo*.

Aşure *has 40 ingredients, including chickpeas, beans and dried fruit.*

Left **Kanyon, Levent** Centre **Glass lamps in the Grand Bazaar** Right **Browsing in the Book Bazaar**

# TOP 10 Shops and Markets

**1 Grand Bazaar (Kapalı Çarşı)** One of the oldest, biggest and most exciting shopping malls in the world, the Grand Bazaar was set up to trade silk, spices and gold in the 15th century – and still sells all three, alongside jazzy glass lampshades, leather jackets and, of course, carpets *(see pp18–19)*.

**Egyptian Bazaar**

**2 Egyptian Bazaar (Mısır Çarşısı)**
Also known as the Spice Bazaar, this is the best place in town to buy little presents, with a sea of spice stalls, piles of Turkish Delight and plenty of cheap and cheerful souvenirs *(see p69)*.

**3 Bağdat Caddesi** This 6-km (3.5-mile) long tree-lined thoroughfare on the Asian side of Istanbul is one of the city's best-known shopping streets. It is home to high-end designer shops, such as Burberry and Dolce & Gabbana, as well as high-street chains, including Zara, GAP and French Connection. You will also find department stores and smaller, independent boutiques here, which cater to most fashion tastes. The area is packed with restaurants, cafés and bars, useful for when weary shoppers need to rest their feet. *Ferry to Kadıköy and then dolmuş to Bostancı*

**4 Book Bazaar (Sahaflar Çarşısı)**
The Book Bazaar started out selling scraps of parchment with Koranic text, but now offers a wide range of antiquarian and second-hand books (including paperbacks) in a variety of languages *(see p70)*.

**5 İstiklal Caddesi** The city's main modern shopping street, İstiklal is packed day and night. If you need a break from sessions hunting for bargain designer clothes (in İş Merkezi) or the perfect glass teacups (in Paşabahçe) there are plenty of cafés to choose from.

**6 Kanyon, Levent** Join the city's most stylish shoppers at Kanyon, Istanbul's biggest and, in some eyes, best shopping mall *(see p83)*.

**7 Nişantaşı** Nişantaşı and neighbouring Teşvikiye are where local fashionistas spend their money on well-known international brands, including Versace and Dior. It is perhaps less exciting for those who can get the same thing at home *(see p83)*.

*If you're buying a large item, shop around to get a sense of prices. When bargaining, take your time and remain polite.*

### 8 İstinye Park

This architecturally impressive luxury shopping mall, which opened in September 2007, is slightly oustide the city centre in the residential area of İstinye. The light-filled corridors lead to shops, restaurants and leisure facilities. Designer shops include Hugo Boss, Louis Vuitton and Turkish boutique chain Vakko. *İstinye Bayırı Cad, No. 73 Sariyer • (0212) 345 55 55 • www.istinyepark.com*

### 9 Arasta Bazaar (Arasta Çarşısı)

This small, upmarket bazaar offers the best souvenir shopping in Sultanahmet. Situated in converted Ottoman stables, it sells good-quality carpets, jewellery and handicrafts in a relatively calm environment, conveniently close to many major sights and hotels *(see pp60, 114)*.

### 10 Çukurcuma, Galatasaray

Many travellers fall in love with this charming old quarter of Beyoğlu, with its eclectic range of antiques and second-hand dealers, whose wares flow out onto the streets around Turnacıbaşı Sokağı. Great for a morning's browsing *(see p83)*.

**Antiques shop, Çukurcuma**

## Top 10 Things to Buy

### 1 Carpets

Carpets *(see pp44–5)* are the true glory of Turkish art – and you can have one on your own hall floor.

### 2 Jewellery

Precious metals are sold by weight, with a mark-up for workmanship. There are plenty of options, including designing your own jewellery.

### 3 Leather

Jackets, bags, wallets and belts are great value and come in all styles, colours and qualities. Again, custom-design if you have enough time.

### 4 Clothes

Shop around and you can find good quality and great design at rock-bottom prices.

### 5 Textiles

Both cottons and silks are made here, and are extremely cheap. Silk scarves are a great-value present.

### 6 Spices

Great heaps of coloured spices are hard to resist. If you buy saffron, check it's the real thing – there's a cheaper alternative (safflower) on sale.

### 7 Historic Reproductions

Reproduction Ottoman miniatures are easy to carry, and look great back home.

### 8 Souvenirs

For fun, buy someone back home pointed slippers or a sparkly belly-dancing outfit.

### 9 Blue Beads

The ubiquitous blue bead is actually a charm to ward off the "evil eye"; believe that or not, they make attractive gifts.

### 10 Food

Turkish Delight, almonds and hazelnuts, honey and all sorts of other comestibles make great presents.

Left **Clear design on reverse side of a silk carpet** Centre **Weaver at work** Right **A *cicim* flat-weave**

# 10 Facts about Turkish Carpets

### 1 Origins

Turkish rug-weaving skills are of ancient origin and have been passed down the generations. They were developed by Central Asian nomads, who used thickly woven goats' hair to make tents, floor coverings and even cradles. This material was portable, warm and virtually waterproof. People soon began to use these weaves as wall decorations.

### 2 Flat-Weaves

A rug is only considered to be a carpet *(hali)* if it has a knotted pile. In flat-weave rugs the vertical (warp) and horizontal (weft) threads are woven flat. *Kilims* are the most basic form, with the design (weft) threads woven into the warp; in *cicims*, a third thread is woven in to create the design, which looks as if it is embroidered. More intricate still are *sumaks*, in which additional design yarns cover the entire surface.

### 3 The Oldest Carpets

*Kilims* have been made in Turkey for around 8,000 years; fragments of pile carpet survive from about 2,000 years ago. The oldest complete carpets in Turkey are 13th-century Seljuk examples made in Konya and Beyşehir in central Anatolia.

### 4 Weaving Materials

The basic materials used for making Turkish carpets are wool, mercerized cotton and pure silk. Most finer carpets have a cotton warp (which forms the base), with a wool or silk weft; flat-weaves are generally made entirely from cotton.

**Hereke carpet**

### 5 Natural Dyes

Cheaper wool or cotton carpets use chemical dyes, but the finest still use traditional natural colours, such as woad or indigo for blues, madder root for shades from brick-red to orange, pinks and purple and camomile, sage and saffron for yellow.

### 6 Hereke Imperial Carpet Factory

The factory at Hereke, 60 km (38 miles) east of Istanbul, was set up in 1843 to provide carpets for the Ottoman court. Its carpets, made from Bursa silk, were larger and more finely woven than any known before.

### 7 Prayer Rugs

Prayer rugs (*namazlık*) usually contain an image of a *mihrab* (prayer niche). The rug was designed to be carried around and laid down in the direction of Mecca for prayers five times a day.



*Look out for felt textiles too – Turkey is the world centre for felt-making, with a tradition going back several hundred years.*

Prayer rug

**8 Symbolism**
Women wove their lives and longings into their carpets. Look for motifs symbolizing good luck (the *elibelinde* or "arms-akimbo" motif), fate (an eight-pointed star), the mother goddess (hands on hips), and heroism (rams' horns).

**9 Number of Knots**
The more knots in a carpet, the denser the weave and the more durable the product – and the clearer the design will appear on the reverse side. A poor quality carpet might have only 9 knots per sq cm (75 per sq inch); a good wool-on-cotton carpet will have 49 knots per sq cm (320 per sq inch); the finest Hereke silk carpet could have an astonishing 400 knots or more per sq cm (2,090 per sq inch) – or 3,240,000 knots per sq m (2,709,030 per sq yd).

**10 Regional Styles**
Carpets used to be made in a profusion of highly distinctive regional styles, but those days are rapidly vanishing as carpet-makers simplify their designs to appeal to the export market.

## Top 10 Tips on Buying a Carpet

**1 Choose Your Location**
Before you travel, decide where you will put your rug, to work out in advance the size and colour you want.

**2 Window-Shop**
Look in a fixed-price store to get an idea of what you like and roughly what it will cost.

**3 Take Your Time**
In the carpet shop, relax – drink tea, and don't feel guilty if the owner gets out every carpet in the shop for you.

**4 Get Knotted**
Check the number of knots – the more, the better.

**5 Beware Chemical Dyes**
Most cheap wool or cotton carpets use chemical dyes, and may be chlorine-bleached to give an aged look. Dab a corner with a damp tissue to see if any dye comes off.

**6 Check the Provenance**
Enquire about the age of the carpet, where it was made, and the traditions in that area.

**7 Haggle**
Start at about half of the original price and work up.

**8 Postage**
Turn down "free" postage. If you carry the rug with you, you can use your duty-free allowance; if it is posted, you will have to pay duty.

**9 Taxes**
An invoice and/or credit-card payment will increase the cost, because the vendor will have to declare the sale for VAT. If you are buying a fully taxed product, get the form to reclaim the tax on departure.

**10 Certification**
All antiquities need a Ministry of Culture certificate for export *(see p109)*.

*A reliable carpet vendor will be happy to give you whatever documentation you need for tax or export purposes.*

Black Eyed Peas, One Love Festival

# TOP 10 Festivals and Events

### 1 International Istanbul Film Festival

Since its inception in 1982, this fortnight-long festival has screened more than 3,000 films from 76 countries. A highlight of the festival is the Award for Lifetime Achievement, instituted in 1996 – winners include French stars Alain Delon and Jeanne Moreau. Most festival screenings are held in cinemas in the vicinity of İstiklal Caddesi. *Various venues • (0212) 334 07 00 • Apr • www.iksv.org*

### 2 Cherry Festival

The pretty village of Polonezköy *(see p52)* celebrates its cherry harvest, as well as its Polish heritage, in the annual Cherry Festival. A unique event in Istanbul, it features Polish song, dance and other cultural events. The festival is by far the busiest time of year in this otherwise peaceful village, which is also known for its honey, flowers and traditional culture. *Jun • www.polonezkoy.com*

### 3 Efes Pilsen One Love Festival

This two-day midsummer extravaganza combines top international acts like Morrissey, Black Eyed Peas and Manu Chao with Turkish rock and dance bands. *Call to check venue • (0212) 334 01 00 • Jul • www.pozitif.info*

### 4 International Istanbul Music and Dance Festival

An impressive array of soloists, ensembles and orchestras has graced the stages of this prestigious festival since it was established in 1973. Mozart's opera The Abduction from the Seraglio is staged each year in Topkapı Palace. *Various venues • (0212) 334 0700 • Jun • www.iksv.org*

Mozart's *Il Seraglio*, International Istanbul Music and Dance Festival

### 5 International Asia-to-Europe Swimming, Rowing and Sailing Competitions

Competitors in this trio of events cross the Bosphorus from a variety of starting points: Kanlıca for swimmers, Arnavutköy for rowers, and Kandilli for yachtsmen. All three races end at Kuruçeşme. Other events include water-skiing, jet-skiing and underwater-swimming displays; folk dancing; and military band performances. *Jul • (0212) 560 0707 • www.bogazici.cc*

Asia-to-Europe Sailing Competition

*Dates for Şeker Bayramı: 8–10 Aug inclusive (2013); 28–30 Jul inclusive (2014)*

Italian jazz band Funk Off perform on İstiklal Caddesi, International Istanbul Jazz Festival

## 6 International Istanbul Jazz Festival

The Jazz Festival's origins lie in a concert by Chick Corea and Steve Kujala at the 1984 Istanbul Music Festival. It was established as an independent event in 1994. The musical range is broad, and you are as likely to encounter Björk or Elvis Costello as you are Brad Mehldau. The choice of venues is eclectic, with traditional clubs, outdoor stages and even a boat cruising on the Bosphorus. *Various venues • (0212) 334 07 00 • Jul • www.iksv.org*

## 7 Istanbul Grand Prix

Istanbul Park, out on the Asian side of the Bosphorus at Tuzla, is a fixture on the Formula 1 Grand Prix calendar. Every August the engines roar to a sell-out crowd of more than 125,000 people, with flights and hotel rooms booking up months in advance. During the rest of the year the park hosts national competitions and minor events, as well as tours of the track for visitors. *Istanbul Park, Tuzla (Asian side) • Aug • Call ahead for tickets (0216) 556 98 00 • www.istanbulparkcircuit.com*

## 8 International Istanbul Fine Arts Biennial

Istanbul's Biennial showcases contemporary visual arts from Turkey and around the globe. Each festival is directed by a curator of a different nationality, who chooses a theme and arranges the programme of exhibitions, conferences and workshops. *Various venues • (0212) 334 07 00 • Sep–Nov, every other year (odd numbers) • www.iksv.org*

## 9 Sugar Festival (Şeker Bayramı)

The Sugar Festival marks the end of the fasting month of Ramazan (Ramadan). People hand out sweets, visit relatives, and enjoy cultural events – and Istanbul's bars and clubs are busy again. Many take advantage of the holiday period by going away for a few days. *Three days, dates vary*

## 10 Feast of Sacrifice (Kurban Bayramı)

Also known as Eid-ul-Adha, the Feast of Sacrifice commemorates the Koranic version of Abraham's sacrifice. It falls two months and ten days after the end of Ramazan. Muslims celebrate by slaughtering a sheep on the morning of the first day of the festival. Friends and family are invited to a lavish meal, but much of the meat goes to charity. Note that this is Turkey's major annual public holiday – nearly everything closes, and the public transport system is seriously stretched. *Four days, dates vary*

*Dates for Kurban Bayramı: 15–18 Oct inclusive (2013); 4–7 Oct inclusive (2014)*

Left **Istanbul Toy Museum** Right **Horse-drawn carriage, Büyükada**

# TOP 10 Activities for Children

## 1 Aqua Club Dolphin

This large water park on the outskirts of the city has plenty of slides and rides. It's ideal for a day cooling off, away from city streets and sightseeing hotspots. *Cemal Paşa Cad, Esenkent • (0212) 672 61 61 • Open 9am–6pm daily (to 7pm in summer) • Adm charge • www.aquaclubdolphin.com*

**Süleymaniye Mosque, Miniatürk**

## 2 Miniatürk

Perfect for children and for tourists in a hurry, Miniatürk packs all Turkey's most important buildings into one beautiful park on the edge of the Golden Horn – at 1:25 scale *(see p73)*.

## 3 Princes' Islands (Adalar)

Take the ferry to Büyükada or Heybeliada, then ride by horse-drawn carriage to the beach for a day of rest and fun. Remember to book the return trip or it can be a long walk *(see p52)*.

## 4 Istanbul Toy Museum (İstanbul Oyuncak Müzesi)

This is one of Istanbul's newest museums, with around 4,000 exhibits – from rag dolls made by Turkish children, to planes, tin toys, model trains and a Wild West gallery *(see p97)*.

## 5 Bosphorus Ferries

Ferries zip back and forth across the Bosphorus, often dodging under the bows of vast tankers and weaving their way past yachts or humble fishing boats. With great views and ultra-cheap prices, they provide some of the best-value entertainment in Istanbul *(see pp28–9, 104)*.

## 6 Turkuazoo

Children will love this giant aquarium with its 90-m (295-ft) underwater tunnel offering visitors a panoramic view of the resident sea creatures. *Forum Shopping Centre, Bayrampaşa, 5km (3 miles) from Atatürk International Airport • (0212) 640 27 40 • Open 10am–6pm Mon–Fri, 10am–8pm Sat–Sun • Adm*

**Scuba diver and fish at Turkuazoo**

*Children with a mechanical turn of mind will also love the Rahmi Koç Museum* **See p74**

7 **Fortress of Europe (Rumeli Hisarı)**
This castle, built by Mehmet the Conqueror in four months in 1452, has plenty of space for children to let off steam – three towers, huge courtyards and an amphitheatre *(see p90)*.

**Mehter Band, Military Museum**

8 **Mehter Band**
For centuries the Mehter Band accompanied the Ottoman army into battle, playing martial music. Today, dressed in their crimson, black and gold uniforms, its members play at the military museum *(see p80)*. It's rousing stuff – loud and entertaining.

9 **Children's Cooking Courses**
Friendly teachers make this a fun half-day activity for children as young as three, accompanied by a parent. *Yıldırım Cad 111, Tahtaminare Mahellesi, Fener • Map L2 • (0212) 534 47 88 • www.istanbulfoodworkshop.com*

10 **Horse Racing and Riding**
The Veliefendi race track has horse racing several times a week. If the kids want to try for themselves, they can be entertained at the Pony Club, where they can ride on the small horses for free. *İstanbul Veliefendi Hipodromu, Ekrem Kurt Bulvarı, Bakırköy • (0212) 444 08 55 • Race meetings mid-Apr to mid-Nov, 2–3 times per week • Adm charge • www.tjk.org*

## Top 10 Green Spaces

1 **Büyük Çamlıca**
Istanbul's highest hill offers wonderful views *(see p98)*.

2 **Maçka Parkı**
Formerly in the grounds of Dolmabahçe Palace. There are a few cafés and, in summer, a small funfair. *Map B5*

3 **Golden Horn Parks**
Since its rehabilitation, the western shore of the Golden Horn has become one long parkland, running from Fener to Eyüp. *Map A4–B5*

4 **Sultanahmet Square**
The large open space around Haghia Sophia and the Blue Mosque merges, via a formal garden with a fountain, into the Hippodrome *(see p60)*.

5 **Gülhane Parkı**
Once the outer grounds of Topkapı Palace, Gülhane Park is today the largest open area in the old city *(see p61)*.

6 **Beykoz Woods (Asian Side)**
While the waterfront village of Beykoz is famous for its glass and for its fish restaurants, the woods behind are a lovely spot for a shady walk. *Map V3*

7 **Belgrade Forest (Belgrat Ormanı)**
This woodland is very popular for picnics *(see p52)*.

8 **Emirgan Parkı**
Emirgan Park hosts the annual Tulip Festival in April *(see p92)*.

9 **Yıldız Parkı**
Yıldız Park was once the grounds of Çırağan Palace *(see pp89, 92)*.

10 **Polonezköy**
This rustic spot, 25 km (16 miles) northeast of Istanbul, is surrounded by a large beech forest, and is popular for walks *(see p52)*.

Left **Leb-i-Derya** Right **Vogue**

# Top 10 Restaurants

## 1 Asitane

The complex flavours of Ottoman court cuisine are resurrected (based on extensive research) at Asitane. Hundreds of years later, almond soup, melon stuffed with minced lamb and goose kebabs are still fit for a sultan *(see p77)*.

## 2 Leb-i-Derya

This is one of the more stylish eateries in the new city, offering cocktails, fabulous food, beautiful people, a stunning view and late-night music. You need to come early to get a seat on the roof terrace *(see p85)*.

## 3 Changa

Food, drink and design come together to create a hip dining experience at this Taksim eatery near the Bosphorus. The fusion menu expertly blends Asian and Mediterranean influences. There's also a great cocktail list with several unusual choices *(see p85)*.

## 4 Seasons Restaurant

The Seasons is the restaurant of the Four Seasons Hotel, which was once an Ottoman prison. Glass rather than thick walls now encloses its pretty courtyard garden. The modern Mediterranean food is imaginative and delicious, and the service is gracious *(see p63)*.

## 5 Feriye Lokantası

Situated in a 19th-century police station on the Bosphorus shore, this fashionable restaurant is taking a fresh look at Turkish cuisine, combining traditional recipes with European flair in one of the most exciting culinary experiences in the city *(see p93)*.

## 6 Vogue

Stick-thin women of extreme beauty sip green apple martinis at this ultra-trendy rooftop restaurant, all white leather and chrome. Chic modernism infuses both the menu and the decor *(see p93)*.

## 7 Mikla

Reserve a terrace table at the Marmara Pera Hotel's stylish rooftop restaurant for the perfect view of the Golden Horn – and of the city, 17 floors below. The Mediterranean cuisine has Turkish and Nordic touches. The decor is elegant – there's even a swimming pool by the bar. A cocktail or two later and you can sink into the soft sofas to recover.

*The Marmara Pera, Meşrutiyet Cad 15, Beyoğlu • Map J5 • (0212) 293 56 56 • $$$$*

**Seasons Restaurant**

*Reservations are advised at all the restaurants listed here.*

## 8 360

Rub shoulders with the swanky young set of Istanbul on 360's superb terrace bar, taking your time to drink in the stunning views of both the Bosphorus and the Golden Horn, then withdraw to the spacious, well-lit interior to sample such eclectic delights as samphire and soya sprouts, Vietnamese beef tartar, polenta-crusted calamari, seafood risotto, lamb loin confit, Margarita sorbet and pistachio *baklava* *(see p84)*.

**View from the terrace, 360**

## 9 Balıkçı Sabahattin

A truly traditional Turkish experience, this wonderful fish restaurant (open since 1927) is situated in an old house with antique carpets and copper pots. There's also an outdoor terrace with lively Gypsy violinists. The food is excellent, although there is no menu – you choose from a wide range of *meze* and the catch of the day *(see p63)*.

## 10 Giritli

Cretan dishes such as ceviche-style sea bass and cracked brine-cured green olives transport diners to their own little Greek island for the night. The fixed-price menu includes drinks, a selection of mezes and perfectly prepared fish. The restored historic house location and pretty restaurant garden are a bonus *(see p63)*.

# Top 10 Entertainment Venues

## 1 Al Jamal

Offers a luxurious evening of top-notch food and belly-dancing *(see p84)*.

## 2 Orient House

Enjoy whirling dervishes and belly dancing at this venue *(see p71)*.

## 3 Babylon

Babylon entertains with its selection of rock, world music and other acts *(see p84)*.

## 4 Cemal Reşit Rey Concert Hall

Daily concerts include Western and Turkish classical, and world music. *Darulbedayi Cad 1, Harbiye • Map B4 • (0212) 231 54 97 • www.crrks.org*

## 5 Aksanat (Akbank) Cultural Centre

This arts centre offers music and theatre. *İstiklal Cad 8 • Map L4 • (0212) 252 35 00 • www.akbanksanat.com*

## 6 Kuruçeşme Arena

Big-name bands perform by the Bosphorus at this open-air arena. *Muallim Naci Cad 60, Kuruçeşme • Map U4 • (0212) 263 39 83 • www.turkcellkurucesmearena.com*

## 7 City Monuments

Try *son-et-lumière* in Sultanahmet Square, or concerts in Haghia Eirene *(see p61)*.

## 8 Nardis Jazz Club

Live jazz performed in an intimate setting *(see p84)*.

## 9 Salon İKSV

Istanbul's top arts organization hosts great classical and jazz concerts *(see p84)*.

## 10 Süreyya Opera House

This Art-Deco-inspired 1920s theatre hosts opera and ballet. *Bahariye Cad 29, Kadıköy • Map U5 • (0216) 346 15 31 • www.sureyyaoperasi.org*

*For more restaurant listings* **See pp63, 71, 77, 85, 93, 99**

Left **Archaeological Museum, İznik** Right **Koza Park, Bursa**

# TOP 10 Excursions from Istanbul

### 1 Princes' Islands (Adalar)

With deserted beaches, pine forests and ancient monasteries, these nine islands in the Sea of Marmara offer a restful break from the city. This is an easy day trip; most ferries from Istanbul (Kabataş) call at the four largest islands – Kınalıada, Burgazada, Heybeliada and Büyükada. On Büyükada and Heybeliada, walking or horse and carriage are the only means of transport – cars are allowed only for essential services. *12 km (8 miles) southeast of Istanbul*

**Harbour of Burgazada, Princes' Islands**

### 2 Yalova

Ferries also run to Yalova, a spa on the southern shore of the Gulf of İzmit. Turks flock here for the hot springs and pools. *24 km (16 miles) southeast of Istanbul*

### 3 Belgrade Forest (Belgrat Ormanı)

Belgrade Forest is the largest area of woodland near Istanbul. Its huge park makes a first-rate spot for family picnics. *20 km (13 miles) north of Istanbul*

### 4 Polonezköy

Polonezköy was established as a Polish enclave in the mid-19th century. Only a few hundred Poles remain today, but the village's history and rural charm live on. Polonezköy is popular with day-trippers for its old wooden houses, the availability of pork (forbidden under Muslim law) and relaxing country walks. *25 km (16 miles) northeast of Istanbul*

### 5 Black Sea Beaches

Kilyos and Şile, both on the Black Sea, are the nearest beaches to Istanbul – and are wonderful for a day trip, although there's not much space on the sands during summer weekends. At Kilyos there are dangerous sea currents, so use only the marked-out areas for swimming. *Kilyos is 27 km (17 miles) from Istanbul; Şile (Asian side) 72 km (45 miles)*

### 6 Gallipoli (Gelibolu)

A one-day tour can take in the major World War I battlefields, memorials and cemeteries in the Gallipoli National Historic Park (Gelibolu Yarımadası Tarihi Milli Parkı); visits can be arranged from Istanbul, Eceabat or Çanakkale. At Anzac Cove (Anzak Koyu) – where thousands of Australians, New Zealanders and Turks were killed in 1915 – Antipodeans gather each 25 April for the Anzac Day memorial service. Book a hotel well in advance. *On the Aegean coast, 350 km (219 miles) west of Istanbul*

*Few İstanbullus refer to Princes' Islands by their full name, Kızıl Adalar (the Red Islands), calling them simply Adalar (the Islands).*

## 7 Edirne

Ottoman capital in the 15th century, Edirne's history includes occupation by Greeks, Bulgarians and Russians. Best known for the Selimiye Mosque, Sinan's 16th-century masterpiece, the town is also noted for its fine Ottoman buildings and the Yağlı Güreş (oil-wrestling) festival, which takes place in summer. *230 km (144 miles) northwest of Istanbul*

**Selimiye Mosque, Edirne**

## 8 Bursa

Historic Bursa is home to some of Turkey's greatest Ottoman architecture, including the mosque and *türbe* (tomb) of Murat I. Also of note are its suburb, Çekirge, famous for its spas, and the nearby Uludağ National Park, the country's most fashionable ski resort. *90 km (60 miles) south of Istanbul*

## 9 Troy (Truva)

Homer's *Iliad* tells of a ten-year siege of the ancient city of Troy by a Greek army in the 13th century BC. Historians assumed Troy was a mythical place until excavations near the Dardanelles – begun by German archaeologist Heinrich Schliemann in the 19th century – uncovered the remains of no fewer than nine cities dating from 3,000 BC onwards, built one on top of one another. Homer's Troy was probably the level called Troy VI (1800–1250 BC) – the most impressive sight is the great wall of Troy VI. *380 km (238 miles) from Istanbul on the Aegean coast • (0286) 283 05 36 • 8:30am–5pm daily • Adm charge*

## 10 İznik

At İznik (known in Roman-Christian times as Nicaea), Emperor Constantine convened a council in AD 325 to produce a unified statement of Christian belief: the Creed of Nicaea. The city was renamed İznik by Orhan Gazi when he captured it in 1331. İznik is famous for its ceramic industry, and especially its painted tiles, which adorn many Ottoman mosques. *87 km (54 miles) southeast of Istanbul*

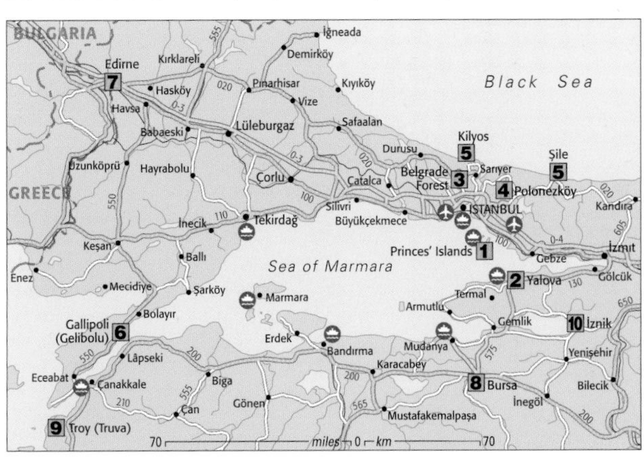


It's best to visit Belgrade Forest on a weekday; the park gets very crowded at weekends, especially in summer.

# AROUND TOWN

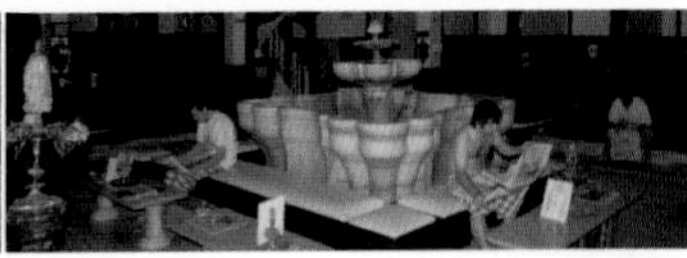

Left **Museum of Turkish and Islamic Arts** Right **Cağaloğlu Baths**

# Sultanahmet and the Old City

MANY OF THE CITY'S GREATEST SIGHTS *are to be found in this historic area, which was in turn the centre of Byzantium, Constantinople and Ottoman Stamboul. Archaeologists have dated settlements in this strategic spot at the entrance to the Golden Horn back to the 6th millennium BC, but recorded history begins around 667 BC, when Greek colonist Byzas founded Byzantion on Seraglio Point (now home to the Topkapı Palace). After his arrival in AD 324, Constantine transformed this port into the dazzling jewel of Constantinople, a new capital for the Roman Empire. By 1453, when the Ottomans seized power, the city was run down and ruinous, and the new rulers stamped their authority – both religious and secular – on its buildings.*

**View of the Blue Mosque**

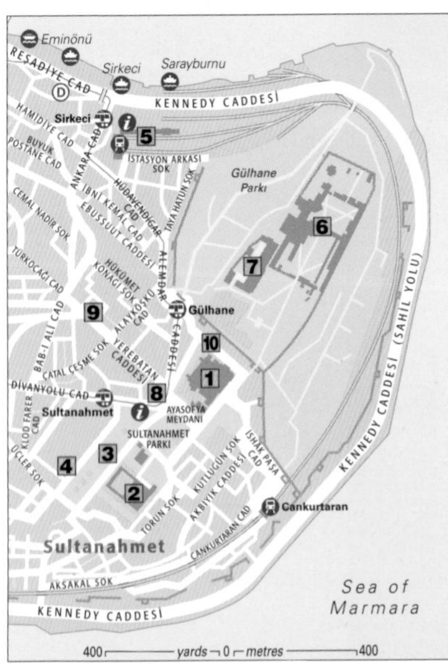


## Top 10 Sights

1. Haghia Sophia
2. Blue Mosque
3. Hippodrome
4. Museum of Turkish and Islamic Arts
5. Sirkeci Station
6. Topkapı Palace
7. Archaeological Museum
8. Basilica Cistern
9. Cağaloğlu Hamamı
10. Soğukçeşme Sokağı

Preceding pages **View across the Sea of Marmara to Asian Istanbul, with the Egyptian Bazaar and the New Mosque in the foreground**

## 1 Haghia Sophia (Ayasofya)

Consecrated by Justinian in 537, the "Church of Holy Wisdom" is an enduring tribute to the skill of its architects, Anthemius of Tralles and Isidore of Miletus, who created a monument that has withstood wars and earthquakes. The scale of its vast central dome was not surpassed until the construction of St Peter's in Rome, 1,000 years later *(see pp12–13)*.

**Haghia Sophia viewed from its gardens**

## 2 Blue Mosque (Sultanahmet Camii)

Begun in 1609, Sultan Ahmet I's mosque was built opposite Haghia Sophia and directly on top of Constantine's Great Palace to stress the supremacy of Islam and the Ottoman Empire over Christian Byzantium *(see pp14–15)*.

## 3 Hippodrome (At Meydanı)

Now a peaceful park, the Hippodrome was the Byzantine chariot racetrack – a stadium capable of holding 100,000 people. Laid out in the 3rd century AD by Emperor Septimus Severus, it was enlarged and connected to the adjacent Great Palace by Constantine. There are three great monuments in the Hippodrome: the Egyptian Obelisk (Dikilitaş) of c.1500 BC, which Constantine transported from Luxor; the Serpentine Column (Yilanlı Sütun) from the Temple of Apollo at Delphi in Greece, made in 479 BC; and the Column of Constantine VII Porphryogenitus (Ormetaş), which is of unknown date and was named after the emperor who had it restored in the 10th century. The stadium once held four great bronze horses, but these were looted by the Crusaders in 1204 and now grace St Mark's Cathedral in Venice. *Map Q5*

**Egyptian Obelisk and Serpentine Column, Hippodrome**

## 4 Museum of Turkish and Islamic Arts (Türk ve İslam Eserleri Müzesi)

This museum is housed in the magnificent palace built by İbrahim Paşa (c.1493–1536), Grand Vizier and son-in-law to Süleyman the Magnificent. It contains a superb collection of more than 40,000 artifacts dating from the 7th century to the present, with exhibits of fine art, crafts, and Turkish domestic life in its evolution from nomad's tent to modern home.

*At Meydanı 46 • Map Q5 • (0212) 518 18 05 • Open 9am–5pm Tue–Sun • Adm charge • www.tiem.gov.tr*

*Stamboul is a variant form of İstanbul. Both names pre-date the Conquest of 1453* (see p32).

## 5 Sirkeci Station (Sirkeci Garı)

Officially opened in November 1890, the glamorous eastern terminus for the Orient Express service was built by German architect August Jachmund, in an eclectic style drawing together elements of Istanbul's varied architectural traditions. The station also houses a railway museum *(see p35)* and a superb restaurant *(see p63)*. Currently, Sirkeci is still the last stop for all trains to Istanbul from Europe; a new tunnel is planned that will connect it with Haydarpaşa on the Asian shore. *İstasyon Cad • Map R2 • (0212) 520 65 75 • Museum open 9am–5pm Tue–Sat • Free*

## 6 Topkapı Palace (Topkapı Sarayı)

The great palace of the Ottoman Empire was both the sultan's residence and the centre of government from 1459 to 1853. The whole complex can take a full day to explore; the highlights are undoubtedly the Harem and the Treasury *(see pp8–11)*.

### Süleyman I

Known to the West as "the Magnificent", Süleyman I preferred the title Kanuni – "the law-giver". Taking the throne aged 26 in 1520, he ruled for 46 years. During that time he doubled the size of the Ottoman Empire and, as caliph (supreme head of the Islamic faith), consolidated Sunni authority over Shia Islam. He also wrote the *Codex Süleymanicus*, which built a comprehensive legal system that defined the concept of justice, and guaranteed equal treatment for all. Süleyman was a great patron of the arts, as well as a poet and goldsmith.

**"Fruit Room", Topkapı Palace Harem**

## 7 Archaeological Museum (Arkeoloji Müzesi)

This is one of the world's great historical museums. It has three principal sections: the Museum of the Ancient Orient, which contains, among other things, the city gates of Babylon; the Tiled Kiosk, with a superb display of ceramics; and the main museum, where royal sarcophagi found at Sidon in Lebanon are star exhibits *(see pp16–17)*.

**Roman statue of Apollo, Archaeological Museum**

## 8 Basilica Cistern (Yerebatan Sarnıcı)

This beautiful "Sunken Palace", as the Turkish name has it, had a prosaic purpose: it was built as a vast underground water-storage tank. Begun by Constantine, it was expanded by Justinian in 532 to ensure that Constantinople was always supplied with water; covering an area of 9,800 sq m (11,720 sq yards), it once held 80 million litres (about 18 million gallons). The cistern roof is supported by 336 pillars, 8 m (26 ft) in height. Look for the upside-down Medusa heads, reused from older Greek buildings. Istanbul's most unusual tourist attraction is also popular as a film location and a venue for concerts. *Yerebatan Cad 13 • Map R4 • (0212) 522 12 59 • Open 9am–6:30pm daily • Adm charge • www.yerebatan.com*

*Sultanahmet is named after Sultan Ahmet I, who commissioned the Blue Mosque (see pp14–15).*

## 9 Cağaloğlu Baths (Cağaloğlu Hamamı)

One of the city's best-known and most picturesque bathhouses, Cağaloğlu Hamamı was built in 1741 by Sultan Mahmut I, with the intention of raising funds to support his library in Haghia Sophia. International figures from King Edward VIII to Kaiser Wilhelm, from Franz Lizst to Florence Nightingale, are all reputed to have bathed here. In more recent times it has been used as a location for countless films and fashion shoots. *Prof Kazım İsmail Gürkan Cad 34 • Map Q3 • (0212) 522 24 24 • Open daily: men, 8am–10pm; women, 8am–8pm • Adm charge • www.cagalogluhamami.com.tr*

## 10 Soğukçeşme Sokağı

This steeply cobbled street, which runs between the outer walls of the Topkapı Palace and Haghia Sophia, is a sequence of pretty Ottoman merchants' homes. The street was restored as part of a 1980s project that was one of the first of its kind in Istanbul. Nine of the houses form the Ayasofya Konakları (see p114), the city's first "special hotel". *Map R4*

**Soğukçeşme Sokağı**

## A Day in Sultanahmet

### Morning

Start your day at the dawn call of the *müezzin*, so that you are ready to visit the **Blue Mosque** as soon as it opens. From there, cross the square to **Haghia Sophia**, then pay a visit to the **Basilica Cistern**, the **Hippodrome** and the **Museum of Turkish and Islamic Arts** before having a gentle stroll through the **Arasta Bazaar** *(see p60)* to the **Mosaics Museum** *(see p60)*. This may sound like too much for a single morning, but the distance between each of these attractions is small, and (aside from the first two) most of the sites are fairly simple. You'll need a little time to relax after this, so choose one of the cafés or restaurants on **Divanyolu** *(see p60)* for lunch, and write a few postcards bought from local vendors.

### Afternoon

Now choose one of two options: either walk across to the **Topkapı Palace** and spend the whole afternoon embroiled in Ottoman court intrigue, mayhem and murder; or wander through the side streets to the **Cağaloğlu Baths** for a Turkish bath before rejoining **Soğukçeşme Sokağı** and making your way to the vast **Archaeological Museum**. When you've had your fill, continue down the hill for a peaceful stroll along the seafront at Eminönü; then take the tram back up the hill to Sultanahmet and choose one of the many wonderful rooftop bars or restaurants from which to watch the sun set over the city and the floodlights playing on Haghia Sophia and the Blue Mosque.

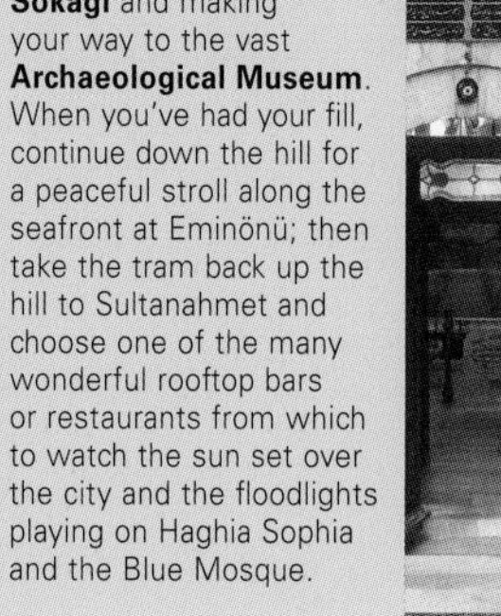

*For more on Turkish baths* **See pp24–5**

Left **Mosaics Museum** Centre **Baths of Roxelana** Right **Calligraphy at the Istanbul Craft Centre**

# TOP 10 Sultanahmet: Best of the Rest

### 1 Sultanahmet Square (Sultanahmet Meydanı)

This leafy square, once the hippodrome of Constantinople, lies between the Blue Mosque and Haghia Sophia. *Map R4*

### 2 The Milion Monument (Milyon Taşi)

The marble pilaster of the Milion can be found in the northern corner of Sultanahmet Square. From the 4th century AD it was used as "point zero" for the measurement of distances to the many cities of the Byzantine Empire. *Haghia Sophia • Map R4*

### 3 Baths of Roxelana (Hürrem Sultan Hamamı)

These baths were built for Süleyman the Magnificent, and are named after the sultan's apparently scheming wife. *Ayasofya Meydanı • Map R4 • (0212) 517 35 35 • Open 8am–10pm daily • www.ayasofyahamami.com*

### 4 Arasta Bazaar (Arasta Çarşısı)

The bazaar was originally built as stables in the 17th century. Around 40 shops sell carpets and other souvenirs. *Map R5 • Open 9am–9pm daily*

### 5 Mosaics Museum (Mozaik Müzesi)

Little remains of Emperor Justinian's vast 6th-century palace but this mosaic floor. *Arasta Bazaar • Map R6 • (0212) 518 12 05 • Open 9am–4:30pm Tue–Sun • Adm charge*

### 6 Istanbul Craft Centre (Caferağa Medresesi)

Watch craftspeople create art, from ceramics to calligraphy, in this 16th-century Koranic college, then take the product home – or sign up for a course yourself. *Caferiye Sok, Soğukkuyu Çıkmazı 1 • Map S5 • (0212) 513 36 01 • Open 9am–7pm Mon–Sat • Free*

### 7 Kaiser Wilhelm Fountain

German Emperor Wilhelm II presented this Neo-Byzantine fountain to Sultan Abdül Hamit II in 1901. *At Meydanı • Map R4*

### 8 Divanyolu Caddesi

Divanyolu was once the *Mese* – the main thoroughfare – of Byzantine Constantinople and Ottoman Stamboul, and continued all the way to the Albanian coast. *Map Q4*

### 9 Cistern of 1001 Columns (Binbirdirek Sarnıcı)

There are in fact only 224 columns in this elegant 4th-century cistern. It is now home to several cafés and hosts live music and events. *Binbirdirek, İmran Öktem Cad 4 • Map Q4 • (0212) 518 10 01 • 9am–9pm daily • Adm charge • www.binbirdirek.com*

### 10 Sultanahmet Hamamı

Enjoy the 17th-century architecture while you are scrubbed clean *(see also pp24–5)*. *Divanyolu Cad, Doktor Emin Paşa Sok No 10 • Map Q4 • (0212) 513 72 04 • www.sultanahmethamami.com*

Left **Sokullu Mehmet Paşa Mosque** Centre **Church of SS Sergius & Bacchus** Right **Church of St John**

# TOP 10 Old City: Best of the Rest

### 1 Haghia Eirene (Aya İrini Kilisesi)

Built in the 6th century on the site of an earlier church, Haghia Eirene was the city's cathedral until Haghia Sophia was built. Later an Ottoman arsenal it is now used for concerts. *Topkapı Palace (1st courtyard) • Map S3 • Open only for concerts and events*

### 2 Imperial Mint (Darphane)

The Ottoman Imperial Mint was founded in 1496. It moved to Topkapı in 1723; today, this complex houses laboratories for the state conservation department and hosts concerts and exhibitions. *Topkapı Palace (1st courtyard) • Map S3*

### 3 History of Islamic Science and Technology Museum

This well laid-out museum exhibits fantastic models of scientific inventions. *Gülhane Park • Map R3 • (0212) 528 80 65 • Open 9am–5pm Wed–Mon • Adm charge • www.ibtav.org*

### 4 Sea Walls

Built in 438 by Cyrus, Prefect of the East, and extended by Theodosius *(see p75)*, the walls are best viewed from the main coastal road. *Kennedy Cad • Map M–S6*

### 5 Bucoleon Palace

Three vast marble windows stare sightlessly out to sea from this last standing fragment of the Great Palace, built into the sea wall. *Kennedy Cad • Map Q6*

### 6 Church of SS Sergius and Bacchus (Küçük Ayasofya Camii)

Known as "Little Haghia Sophia", this church was built in 527 and converted into a mosque in 1500. The marble columns and carved frieze with a Greek inscription are original. *Küçük Ayasofya Camii Sok • Map P6*

### 7 Kumkapı

The old Byzantine harbour is now a huddle of lively fish restaurants *(see p63)*. *Map M6*

### 8 Sokollu Mehmet Paşa Mosque

Built by Sinan for Grand Vizier Sokollu Mehmet Paşa, this lovely mosque behind the Hippodrome contains some fine İznik tiles, an elaborately painted ceiling and four tiny black stones from the Kaaba in Mecca. *Camii Kebir Sok • Map P5 • 9:30am–4:30pm Tue–Sun; may need the keyholder to see inside the mosque*

### 9 Yedikule Castle

This Ottoman fortress is built onto a section of the Theodosian Walls *(see p75)*. *Yedikule Meydanı Sok • Bus 31, 80, 931 • Open 9am–4:30pm Thu–Tue • Adm charge*

### 10 Church of St John of Studius (İmrahor Camii)

Only the outer walls remain of this once-great monastery, built in 463. It was one of the Byzantine Empire's main centres of scholarship. *İmam Aşir Sok • Free*

Left **Çorlulu Ali Paşa Medresesi** Centre **Café Meşale** Right **Sultan Pub**

# TOP 10 Bars, Cafés and Casual Eateries

**1 Çorlulu Ali Paşa Medresesi**
Lounge on cushions in one of several atmospheric tea-shops with locals puffing on the *nargile*. No alcohol. *Divanyolu 36 • Map Q4*

**2 Doy-doy**
This cheap and cheerful place has a good selection of kebabs, pizza, salads and vegetarian options. No alcohol. *Sifa Hamamı Sok 13 • Map Q6*

**3 Sultanahmet Köftecisi**
A long-lived local institution, this superb source of affordable, delicious Turkish food, right on Sultanahmet Square, has now been surrounded by other cafés with suspiciously similar names. Make sure you find the right one! *Divanyolu 12 • Map Q4*

**4 Lale (The Pudding Shop)**
Once an essential stop on the "Hippy Trail", with a message board and copious quantities of cheap food, Lale has lost a little atmosphere but is still great for backpackers. The food is good value, the service is friendly, and they offer draught beer and free Wi-Fi. *Divanyolu Cad 6 • Map Q4*

**5 Sultan Pub**
This is the epitome of modern Istanbul – an excellent rooftop restaurant, a pub with TV blaring sports downstairs, a pavement café (great cappuccinos and cakes), a souvenir shop and a Byzantine cistern as a basement. *Divanyolu Cad 2 • Map Q4*

**6 Café Camille**
This lovely café, just off the main drag, provides a very welcome respite from sight-seeing with its coffee drinks, fresh juices, salads and other delicious light bites. *Çatalçeşme Sok 2, off Bab-i Ali Cad 36 • Map Q4*

**7 Çiğdem Pastanesi**
Enjoy traditional Turkish tea or a well-made cappuccino with plenty of creamy froth at this classic patisserie. If you're in the mood for a light snack, the sticky, honey-drenched baklava is a local favourite. *Divanyolu Cad 62 • Map Q4*

**8 Café Meşale**
A quiet place for a cup of tea and *nargile* during the day, in the evening Café Meşale becomes a restaurant with live music and Whirling Dervish performances. *Arasta Bazaar • Map Q5*

**9 Cheers**
Space may be at a premium here, but there are large beers – also loud music, low prices and crowds of travellers swapping tall tales. The shady pavement tables are a good place to relax at midday. *Akbıyık Cad 20 • Map R5*

**10 Yeşil Ev Beer Garden**
Part of the Yeşil Ev Hotel, this delightful garden bar with a glassed conservatory offering coffee, cakes and alcohol is a great place to chill out. *Kabasakal Cad 5 • Map R5*

Balıkçı Sabahattin

**Price Categories**

For a typical meal of *meze* and main course for one without alcohol, and including taxes and extra charges.

| | |
|---|---|
| $ | under $7 |
| $$ | $7–13 |
| $$$ | $13–18 |
| $$$$ | $18–28 |
| $$$$$ | over $28 |

# Top 10 Restaurants

### 1 Sarnıç

The atmosphere is fabulous in this romantically converted Byzantine cistern serving Turkish/French cuisine. Book ahead. *Soğukçeşme Sok • Map R4 • (0212) 512 42 91 • $$$$*

### 2 Orient Express

This cavernous 19th-century Gothic station restaurant *(see p58)* offers surprisingly good traditional Turkish food. *Platform 2, Sirkeci Station • Map Q2 • (0212) 522 22 80 • $$$*

### 3 Giritli

Fine fish and a bountiful array of unusual mezes are the stars at this Cretan-style eatery. *Keresteci Hakkı Sok 8 • Map R6 • (0212) 458 22 70 • $$$$$*

### 4 Buhara 93 Restaurant

Turkish kebabs and pizza are a speciality here, and there's a large garden where you can enjoy live music. *Nakil Bent Sok 15/A • Map Q6 • (0212) 518 15 11 • $$$*

### 5 Amedros

By day this is a friendly café. In the evening it becomes a bistro serving Turkish and European food, with good vegetarian options. *Hoca Rüstem Sok 7, off Divanyolu • Map Q4 • (0212) 522 83 56 • $$*

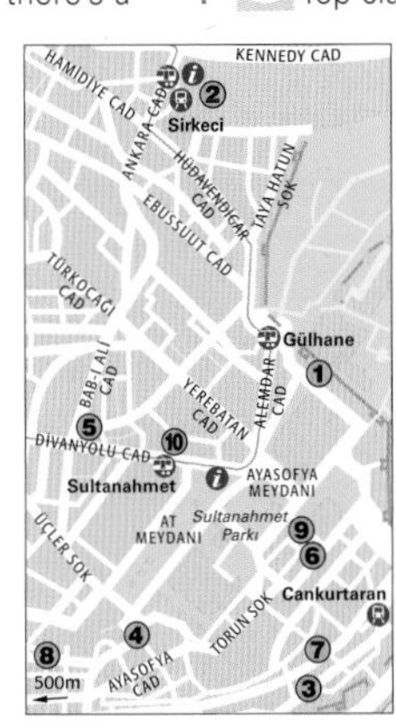


### 6 Restaurant en la Luna

Go native in this quiet back-street restaurant. The mainly Turkish food is excellent and copious, and the staff are friendly. *Utangaç Sok 23 • Map R5 • (0212) 518 72 67 • $$$*

### 7 Balıkçı Sabahattin

One of the city's finest fish restaurants since 1927. Head here for a special night out. *Seyit Hasankuyu Sok 1, off Cankurtaran Cad • Map R5 • (0212) 458 18 24 • $$$$*

### 8 Kumkapı

There are many *meyhanes* (taverns) to choose from in this old fishing neighbourhood, serving fresh fish and *meze* washed down with *rakı*. Musicians play traditional *fasil* to the tables and expect to be tipped. *Map M6 • $$*

### 9 Seasons Restaurant

Top-class contemporary European cuisine with a hint of Asian fusion. *Four Seasons Hotel, Tevfikhane Sok 1 • Map R5 • (0212) 402 30 00 • $$$$$*

### 10 Rumeli Café

This popular restaurant in an old printing factory serves a Turkish and Mediterranean menu. Good vegetarian options. *Ticarethane Sok 8 • Map Q4 • (0212) 512 00 08 • $$$*

*Note that price indications for restaurants and cafés in this guide are given in US dollars*

Left **Spices in the Egyptian Bazaar** Right **İznik tiles, Rüstem Paşa Mosque**

# Bazaar Quarter and Eminönü

IN 1453, FOLLOWING HIS CONQUEST OF *Constantinople, Sultan Mehmet II chose this area, close to the Graeco-Roman Forum of the Bulls, as the place to begin construction of a model city based on Islamic principles. The key ingredients were mosques and* medreses *(religious schools), charitable institutions, accommodation for travellers, and a Grand Bazaar – the latter funding all the others and a great deal more besides. All these were constructed – and many still remain – in one of the city's most fascinating and vibrant districts, where you can buy, with equal ease, a plastic bucket and an antique silk carpet, an ancient religious text or a kilo of peppercorns.*

**Waterfront scene at Eminönü**

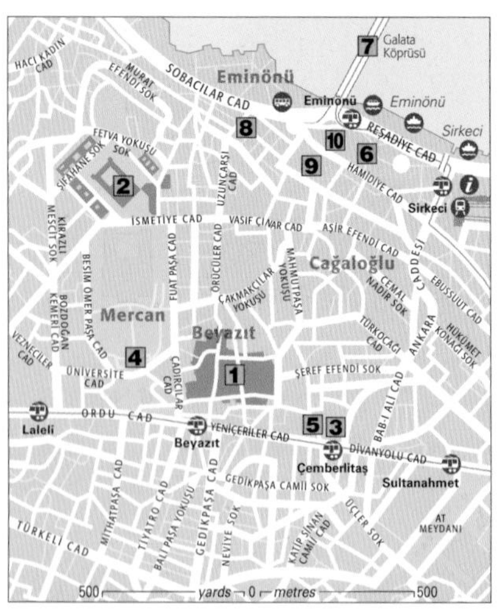


## Top 10 Sights

1. Grand Bazaar
2. Süleymaniye Mosque
3. Çemberlitaş Baths
4. Beyazıt Square
5. Constantine's Column
6. Eminönü
7. Galata Bridge
8. Rüstem Paşa Mosque
9. Egyptian Bazaar
10. New Mosque



Preceding pages **Interior view of the Süleymaniye Mosque**

## 1 Grand Bazaar (Kapalı Çarşı)

Shoppers in the Grand Bazaar

The bazaar was one of the first institutions established by Mehmet the Conqueror after 1453. Its oldest part is the domed İç Bedesten, a lockable warehouse used for trading and storing the most valuable wares. Today, as well as covered streets containing thousands of shops and stalls, there are cafés, restaurants, tea houses, water fountains and even ATM machines – all designed to keep you browsing and buying for as long as possible. There are also several *hans* – originally travellers' inns, now mostly workshops and small factories *(see pp18–19)*.

## 2 Süleymaniye Mosque (Süleymaniye Camii)

The Süleymaniye Mosque, built for Süleyman I in 1550–57, is the largest and most lavish in the city. Süleyman and his wife Roxelana are both buried here, while the great Mimar Sinan, architect of the mosque, is buried just outside the main complex in a tomb he designed and built himself *(see pp20–21)*.

Süleymaniye Mosque

## 3 Çemberlitaş Baths (Çemberlitaş Hamamı)

Nur Banu, wife of the drunken Selim the Sot (son of Süleyman and Roxelana), commissioned these baths from Sinan in 1584. In those days they were run as a charitable foundation; today they are distinctly more upmarket. Their gracious domed halls make them a popular tourist attraction *(see pp24–5)*.

## 4 Beyazıt Square (Beyazıt Meydanı)

This grand open space has been one of the city's principal meeting places for centuries. Popularly known as Beyazıt Square, its official name is Freedom Square (Hürriyet Meydanı). It stands on the site of the Graeco-Roman *Forum Tauri* (Forum of the Bulls), which was extended by Emperor Theodosius in 393. The forum gained its name from the bronze bull at its centre, a place of sacrifice in the pre-Christian era. Some of its colonnades, carved in the form of peacock feathers, were reused in the building of the Basilica Cistern *(see p58)*, while others lie abandoned along the tram tracks on Ordu Caddesi. Part of the Column of Theodosius is built into the foundations of Beyazıt Hamamı (now shops). The square hosts a daily flea market, and is home to the Beyazıt Mosque, Istanbul University and the Museum of Calligraphy *(see p70)*. *Map M3*

Fishing on the Galata Bridge

## 5 Constantine's Column (Çemberlitaş)

Built of Egyptian porphyry, this column, 35 m (115 ft) tall, once stood in the centre of the Forum of Constantine, topped with a statue of Constantine dressed as the god Apollo. It was erected as part of the inauguration of the Roman Empire's new capital in 330. Constantine buried holy relics – said to have included the axe Noah used to build his ark – around the base. Its Turkish name, Çemberlitaş (Hooped Column), refers to the reinforcing metal hoops added in 416 and renewed in 1701. *Divanyolu Cad • Map P4*

Constantine's Column

### Emperor Constantine

The son of a leading army officer, Constantine (c.280–337) became one of a triumvirate of rulers of the Roman Empire. In 312, following a religious vision, he defeated his main rival, Maxentius, while fighting under the sign of the Christian cross. On becoming sole emperor in 324 he declared Christianity the state religion. In 325 he called the Council of Nicaea, which laid down the basic tenets of the faith. In 330 he inaugurated his new capital, Constantinople. On his deathbed, he formally converted to Christianity, and was buried at the city's Church of the Holy Apostles *(see p73)*.

## 6 Eminönü

From the Grand Bazaar, steep alleys crowded with market stalls lead down through Tahtakale to the Eminönü waterfront. It's a great place to roam, with mosques and markets, Byzantine warehouses, street sellers offering everything from pretzels to fake watches, and a bank of piers with ferries to every part of the city, all split by the swirl of traffic along the dual carriageway that leads around the coast. *Map N1*

## 7 Galata Bridge (Galata Köprüsü)

The predecessor of this modern bridge across the Golden Horn was an iron pontoon structure of 1909–12. It was underequipped for modern traffic, and its pontoons, by blocking water flow, trapped pollution in the Golden Horn. It was replaced in 1992 by the current two-level concrete bridge. The city views from the upper level, especially at sunset, are breathtaking; the old bridge, initially used as a footbridge near Hasköy, was later demolished by city authorities. *Map F3*

## 8 Rüstem Paşa Mosque (Rüstem Paşa Camii)

This enchanting mosque was built by Sinan in 1561. It was commissioned by Süleyman the Magnificent's daughter Mihrimah in memory of her husband, Rüstem Paşa, Süleyman's Grand Vizier. The mosque blazes with richly coloured İznik tiles, inside and out, while galleries and windows flood the hall with light. *Hasırcılar Cad • Map N1 • (0212) 526 73 50 • Open 9am–dusk daily • Free*

## 9 Egyptian Bazaar (Mısır Çarşısı)

This marketplace was built in 1660 as part of the New Mosque complex. Its name derives from the fact that it was originally financed by duties on Egyptian imports, although it is better known in English as the Spice Bazaar because for centuries, spices were the main goods sold here. These days, the bazaar has given itself over entirely to satisfying the tourist trade – it's the best place to buy small presents from *lokum* (Turkish Delight) to phials of saffron, from pistachios and almonds to incense or coffee. Belly-dancing outfits are also available. *Eminönü • Map P1 • Open 8am–7pm Mon–Sat*

## 10 New Mosque (Yeni Cami)

This large, rather gloomy mosque was commissioned in 1597 by Valide Sultan Safiye, mother of Sultan Mehmet III. Work was interrupted when the architect was executed for heresy and Safiye was banished after her son's death. It was completed in 1663 by Valide Sultan Turhan Hayice, mother of Sultan Mehmet IV. The interior is richly decorated but has relatively poor-quality İznik tiles. Beside the mosque are the tombs of Valide Sultan Turhan Hatice, Mehmet IV, five other sultans and many princes and princesses.

*Eminönü • Map P1 • (0212) 527 85 05 • Open 9am–dusk daily • Free*

**Interior of the New Mosque**

## A Day's Shopping

### Morning

Start the day clean and refreshed following a visit to the **Çemberlitaş Baths**, then pop into the **Nuruosmaniye Mosque** *(see p70)* before getting down to the real business of the day in the **Grand Bazaar**. Depending on how much time and money you spend here, either have lunch at one of the cafés in the Bazaar or walk on through **Beyazıt Square** and down the hill to the **Süleymaniye Mosque** to pay your respects at the tombs of Süleyman and Roxelana. If you didn't eat earlier, lunch at the Darüzziyafe Restaurant *(see p71)*, or at one of the cafés next to the mosque.

### Afternoon

Leave the mosque along İsmetiye Caddesi, turn left into Uzunçarşı Caddesi and head down the hill through crowded market streets, where metal- and woodworkers still ply their trade, before turning right on Tahtakale Caddesi, a sensory treat with its traditional spice and coffee sellers. Carry on downhill and eventually you will end up in Eminönü, where you can visit the **Rüstem Paşa Mosque** and look at the **New Mosque** before a last round of shopping – if you have the stamina – in the **Egyptian Bazaar**. Between the New Mosque and the Egyptian Bazaar is the market for flowers, plants, seeds and songbirds. Have dinner at Hamdi Et Lokantası *(see p71)* or the Orient Express in Sirkeci Station *(see p63)* – or take the tram back up to Sultanahmet and rooftop views of the sunset.

Left **Kalenderhane Mosque** Centre **Istanbul University** Right **Nuruosmaniye Mosque**

# TOP 10 Best of the Rest

### 1 Book Bazaar (Sahaflar Çarşısı)

Manuscripts have been traded in this courtyard since medieval times, although printed books were banned until 1729. Now the market sells antiquarian books and second-hand paperbacks. *Sahaflar Çarşısı Sok • Map M4*

### 2 Museum of Calligraphy (Türk Vakıf Hat Sanatları Müzesi)

In a culture that forbade the use of the human image, calligraphy was a high art. On display are manuscripts, tools and a tableau of an early workshop. *Beyazıt Meydanı • Map M4 • (0212) 527 58 51 • Closed for renovation, phone for opening times • Adm charge*

### 3 Beyazıt Tower (Beyazıt Kulesi)

This elegant marble tower, built in 1828 as a fire lookout, stands in the grounds of Istanbul University. *Ordu Cad • Map M3 • Closed to the public*

### 4 Beyazıt Mosque (Beyazıt Camii)

Built in 1506 by Beyazıt II, this is the oldest surviving imperial mosque in Istanbul. *Yeni Maharet Cad • Map M4 • (0212) 212 09 22*

### 5 Atik Ali Paşa Mosque (Atik Ali Paşa Camii)

This 15th-century copy of the original Fatih Mosque is named after its builder, Grand Vizier to Beyazıt II. *Yeniçeriler Cad • Map P4*

### 6 Tulip Mosque (Laleli Cami)

The Tulip Mosque was built by Mustafa III in 1763, with lavish use of coloured marble in the new Ottoman Baroque style. Mustafa is buried here. *Ordu Cad • Map D5 • Open prayer times only*

### 7 Nuruosmaniye Mosque (Nuruosmaniye Camii)

Completed by Sultan Osman III in 1748, Nuruosmaniye was the first Baroque mosque in the city. *Vezirhanı Cad • Map P4*

### 8 Kalenderhane Mosque (Kalenderhane Camii)

The original 5th-century bathhouse on this site was converted in the 9th century into the Monastery of Maria Kyriotissa, then into a mosque. Don't miss the superb Byzantine marble in the prayer hall. *16 Mart Şehitleri Cad • Map E5 • Open prayer times only*

### 9 Bodrum Mosque (Bodrum Camii)

A working mosque since 1500, this was originally a Byzantine monastery, founded by Admiral Romanus Lecapenus. *Sait Efendi Sok • Map D5 • Open prayer times only*

### 10 Istanbul University

Founded in 1863, the university moved to its present campus in 1866. Security is very tight, but it is usually possible to walk through the grounds during the working week. *Beyazıt Meydanı • Map M2–3 • (0212) 440 00 00*

*Beyazıt Tower was built on the site of Mehmet the Conqueror's original palace, which burnt to the ground in 1541.*

Havuzlu Lokantası

**Price Categories**

For a typical meal of *meze* and main course for one without alcohol, and including taxes and extra charges.

| | |
|---|---|
| $ | under $7 |
| $$ | $7–13 |
| $$$ | $13–18 |
| $$$$ | $18–28 |
| $$$$$ | over $28 |

# Top 10 Cafés and Restaurants

### 1 Pandeli

Occupying a gorgeous, domed, İznik-tiled dining room above the Spice Market, Pandeli has been an Istanbul institution since it opened in 1901. Book in advance. *Mısır Çarşısı 1 • Map P1 • (0212) 527 39 09 • $$$*

### 2 Café Ay

Rest your weary feet and enjoy coffee or a sandwich at this café inside the Grand Bazaar. *Takkeciler Sok 41–5, Kapalı Çarşı • Map N3 • (0212) 527 98 53 • $*

### 3 Darüzziyafe

Once the soup kitchen of the Süleymaniye Mosque, this atmospheric restaurant serves first-rate Ottoman food. No alcohol. *Şifahane Cad 6 • Map M2 • (0212) 511 84 14 • $$$*

### 4 Havuzlu Lokantası

This is the best of the simple restaurants in the covered bazaar, with excellent kebabs and *meze* served to the traders as well as the shoppers. Arrive early – it can get crowded. *Gani Çelebi Sok 3, Kapalı Çarşı • Map N3 • (0212) 527 33 46 • Open lunch only, closed Sun • $*

### 5 Tarihi Kuru Fasulyeci

This restaurant has been serving up simple, hearty Ottoman cuisine for 80 years. Its speciality is rice and beans, slowly cooked. A good lunch stop. *Süleymaniye Cad, Prof Siddik Sami Onar Cad 11 • Map M2 • (0212) 513 62 19 • No credit cards • $*

### 6 Asmalı Konak

The *testi kebap* – chicken or lamb cooked in a sealed clay pot – is delicious. *Biçki Yurdu Sok 29/30 • Map Q4 • (0212) 514 45 56 • $$$$*

### 7 Hamdi Et Lokantası

Specialities include *erikli kebap* (minced suckling lamb). *Kalçın Sok 17, Tahmis Cad • Map P1 • (0212) 528 03 90 • $$*

### 8 Café Mimar Sinan

A favourite with students, with kilim-covered benches outdoors. *Süleymaniye Cad, Prof Siddik Sami Onar Cad 37/43, Tiryakiler Çarşısı • Map M2 • $$*

### 9 Orient House

A cultural evening offers dinner, Turkish music and belly dancing. *Tiyatro Cad 25/A, Beyazıt • Map M5 • (0212) 517 61 63 • $$$$$*

### 10 Kofteci Ramiz

Part of a chain, this grill and self-service salad bar serves good quality kofte and other grilled meats, as well as soups and desserts. No alcohol. *Bab-i Ali Cad • Map Q4 • (0212) 527 13 40 • $$*

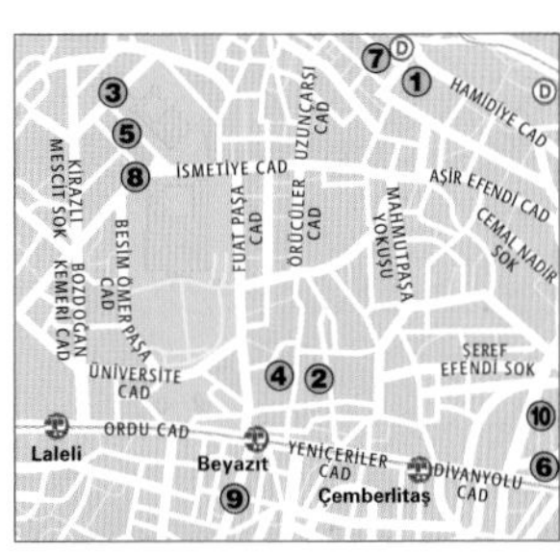

Left **Church of Pammakaristos** Centre **Parecclesion dome, Church of St Saviour** Right **Miniatürk**

# The Golden Horn, Fatih and Fener

THE GOLDEN HORN, A FJORD-LIKE RIVER INLET *that divides the old and new cities of European Istanbul, is enjoying a new lease of life. A major clean-up campaign, including the construction of a huge fountain to oxygenate the water, has begun to banish the foul-smelling pollution that for many years drove people from the area. As a result, run-down Fener and Balat are being eyed greedily by developers, the old-city shore has miles of parks and walkways, and the new-city shore is home to attractions such as Miniatürk and the Rahmi Koç Museum. The Turkish Navy's decision to move out of the old Jewish neighbourhood of Hasköy in 2007 left another area ripe for development.*

**Pierre Loti Café**

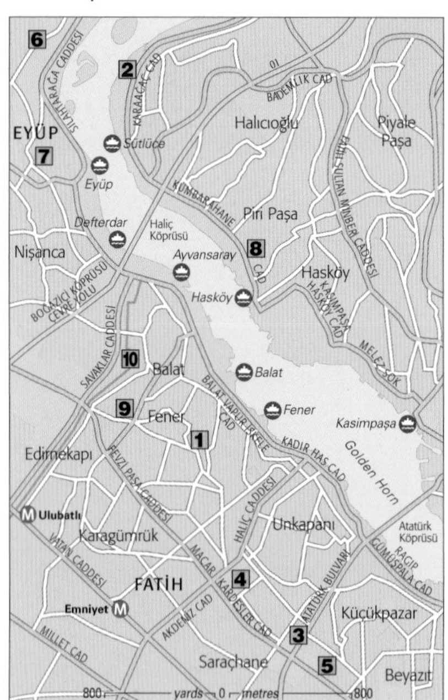


## Top 10 Sights

1 Church of Pammakaristos
2 Miniatürk
3 Aqueduct of Valens
4 Fatih Mosque
5 Prince's Mosque
6 Pierre Loti
7 Eyüp Sultan Mosque
8 Rahmi Koç Museum
9 Church of St Saviour in Chora
10 Theodosian Walls

## 1 Church of Pammakaristos (Fethiye Camii)

Built by Emperor John II Comnenus in the 12th century, this was the headquarters of the Greek Orthodox Patriarchate from 1456 to 1568. The church was later converted into a mosque, and in 1591 renamed *Fethiye* (Victory) to celebrate Murat III's conquest of present-day Georgia and Azerbaijan. The side-chapel is now a museum, containing a wonderful series of Byzantine mosaics – some of the finest in Istanbul. *Fethiye Kapısı • Map K3 • Open 9am–5pm daily • Adm charge*

## 2 Miniatürk

Here's a chance to take in all of Turkey's finest sights in a single afternoon – this intriguing park on the shore of the Golden Horn contains 1:25 scale models of the country's most impressive structures, from the Bosphorus Bridge to Haghia Sophia. Other attractions include a miniature railway, model cars and boats, a cinema, a maze and a playground. *İmrahor Cad, Sütlüce • Map T4 • (0212) 222 28 82 • Open 9am–7pm daily (9pm in high season) • Adm charge • www.miniaturk.com.tr*

Aqueduct of Valens

## 3 Aqueduct of Valens (Bozdoğan Kemeri)

West of Süleymaniye are the near-perfect remains of the two-storey aqueduct built by Emperor Valens in 368. Repaired many times in the intervening years, the aqueduct remained in use until the 19th century, bringing water from the Belgrade Forest to the centre of the Great Palace complex, near the Hippodrome. *Atatürk Bulvarı (north side of Saraçhane Parkı) • Map D4*

## 4 Fatih Mosque (Fatih Camii)

This huge Baroque mosque is the third major building to have occupied this site. The first was the Church of the Holy Apostles (burial place of many Byzantine emperors, including Constantine). Mehmet the Conqueror then constructed Istanbul's first great imperial mosque on the church's crumbling remains, but his building was destroyed in an earthquake in 1766. Today's mosque was built mainly in the 18th century by Sultan Mustafa III. It contains the tombs both of Mehmet the Conqueror and of his wife Gülbahar Hatun. Every Wednesday there is a busy street market outside. *Fevzi Paşa Cad • Map C3–4 • Open 9am–dusk daily • Free*

Fatih Mosque

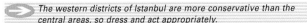

*The western districts of Istanbul are more conservative than the central areas, so dress and act appropriately.*

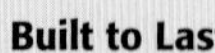

**Built to Last**

There are 11 fortified gates and 192 towers in the Theodosian Walls. The outer wall is 2 m (6 ft) thick and 8.5 m (28 ft) tall, separated from the 5-m- (16-ft-) thick, 12-m- (39-ft-) high inner wall by a 20 m (66 ft) moat. The walls of Byzantium were built to withstand anything, and did so for 1,000 years. When, finally, they were breached in 1453, the last Byzantine Emperor, Constantine IX, vanished into history, last seen fighting on the wall itself.

### 5 Prince's Mosque (Şehzade Camii)

This elegant mosque and complex of *medrese*, courtyard, tombs and *imaret* (soup kitchen) was built by Süleyman the Magnificent in honour of his son Prince Mehmet. It is one of the first imperial designs by the great architect Sinan *(see p21)*. The tomb of Helvacı Baba is a popular pilgrimage destination. *Şehzade Başı Cad 70, Saraçhane • Map D4 • Open daily (tombs open 9am–5pm Tue–Sun) • Free*

### 6 Pierre Loti

During his time in Istanbul, Pierre Loti – the pseudonym and nom de plume of French sailor, author and Turkophile Julien Viaud – frequented a café in Eyüp, and the surrounding area is now named after him. Arriving in the city in 1876, Viaud fell in love with a local woman whose name he gave to the title of his novel, *Aziyade*, which chronicles their difficult relationship. The area known as Pierre Loti Hill can be painlessly visited via the cable car, from beside Eyüp Mosque. The fantastic views of the Golden Horn are best admired from the hilltop Pierre Loti Café *(see p77)*.

### 7 Eyüp Sultan Mosque (Eyüp Sultan Camii)

Istanbul's holiest mosque was built by Mehmet the Conqueror in 1458, over the *türbe* (burial site) of the Prophet Mohammed's friend and standard-bearer, Eyüp el-Ensari, whose tomb opposite is the third holiest pilgrimage site in Islam (after Mecca and Jerusalem). The mosque courtyard, where the coronations of Ottoman sultans took place, has intricately painted İznik tiles, and is usually filled with worshippers queuing to pay their respects. *Eyüp Meydanı (off Camii Kebir Cad) • Map A4 • (0212) 564 73 68 • Tomb open 9:30am–4:30pm • Donations*

**Eyüp Sultan Mosque**

### 8 Rahmi Koç Museum (Rahmi Koç Müzesi)

This eclectic museum is named after its founder, the industrialist Rahmi Koç. The main part of the collection – a magnificent assortment of vintage cars, steam engines, motorbikes, boats, the imperial railway carriage of Sultan Abdül Aziz, and much more besides – is situated in a 19th-century shipyard building. Outside are aircraft, boats, restored shops and a submarine. Across the

*Eyüp Sultan Mosque was flattened in the earthquake of 1766 and rebuilt in 1800.*

road, in a restored Ottoman anchor foundry with Byzantine foundations, are model engines, trains, cars and more boats. There is also an excellent café *(see p77)* and the gourmet Halat Restaurant. ⊗ *Hasköy Cad 5-27 • Map B5 • (0212) 369 66 00 • Open 10am–5pm Tue-Fri, 10am–7pm Sat, Sun • Adm charge • www.rmk-museum.org.tr*

## 9 Church of St Saviour in Chora (Kariye Camii)

First a church, then a mosque, now a museum, the Church of St Saviour in Chora was built in the late 11th century and restored in the early 14th by Theodore Metochites, who also commissioned the superb series of mosaics and frescoes that he hoped would secure him "a glorious memory among posterity till the end of the world" *(see p22–3)*.

## 10 Theodosian Walls (Teodos II Surları)

Built by Emperor Theodosius II in 412–22 and partially restored, the walls enclosing the old city from the Sea of Marmara (Yedikule) to the Golden Horn (Ayvansaray) are startlingly intact. You can walk sections, especially at Yedikule *(see p61)*, although some isolated stretches are not safe to visit alone. The moat has been turned into one long vegetable garden. ⊗ *Map A5*

**Theodosian Walls**

## A Day along the Golden Horn

### Morning

Start the morning at **Fatih Mosque**; look out for the tombs of Sultan Mehmet and his wife behind the prayer hall. Walk down to Fener to see the **Church of St George** at the **Greek Patriarchate** *(see p76)*, then cut through Fener's backstreets to reach **St Mary of the Mongols** *(see p76)*. Admire the Byzantine mosaics in the museum section of the **Church of Pammakaristos** and then head towards Edirnekapı to see the mosaics and frescoes at the **Church of St Saviour in Chora**. Take a well deserved break and feast on Ottoman culinary delights at **Asitane Restaurant** *(see p77)*, with a strong Turkish coffee to boost your energy levels.

### Afternoon

Have a look at the remarkable **Theodosian Walls** before heading down to explore the streets of **Balat** *(see p76)* and pay a visit to **Ahrida Synagogue** – Istanbul's oldest. Walk along the seafront to Eyüp and join the queues paying their respects at the tomb of Eyüp Ensari in the **Eyüp Sultan Mosque**. If your legs are starting to tire, jump into the **cable car** to **Pierre Loti**, but better still, walk uphill through **Eyüp Cemetery** *(see p76)* and have a cup of tea or two – while admiring the views – at the **Pierre Loti Café** *(see p77)*. If you chose to skip lunch – or perhaps even if you didn't – then dine in style at **Aziyade Restaurant** *(see p77)* for a perfect end to the day.

Left **Church of St Stephen of the Bulgars** Centre **Eyüp Cemetery** Right **Church of the Pantocrator**

# Top 10 Best of the Rest

### 1 Church of the Pantocrator (Molla Zeyrek Camii)

This fine, sadly decayed Byzantine church, now a mosque, is all that remains of a once-powerful monastery. *İbadethane Sok, Küçükpazar • Map D3 • (0212) 532 50 23 • Bus 28, 61B, 87 • Open 20 mins before and after prayer times • Small tip*

### 2 Aynalı Kavak Palace (Aynalı Kavak Kasrı)

This 17th-century Ottoman palace has an exhibition of Turkish musical instruments. *Kasımpaşa Cad, Hasköy • Map D1 • (0212) 250 40 94 • Bus 47, 54 • Open 9:30am–4pm daily except Mon & Thu • Adm charge*

### 3 Church of St Stephen of the Bulgars (Bulgar Kilisesi)

The body of this late-19th-century church was entirely prefabricated in Vienna, in cast iron. *Mürsel Paşa Cad 85, Balat • Map L2 • Bus 55T, 99A • Open 9am–5pm daily • Free*

### 4 Rose Mosque (Gül Camii)

The Rose Mosque was originally the 9th-century Church of St Theodosia. *Vakıf Mektebi Sok 16, Fatih • Map D2 • (0212) 534 34 58 • Open prayer times • Small tip*

### 5 Church of St George (Aya Yorgi)

This church is the centre of the worldwide headquarters of the Greek Orthodox Church. *Sadrazam Ali Paşa Cad 35, Fener • Map L2 • (0212) 525 54 16 • Bus 55T, 99A • Open 9am–5pm daily • Free*

### 6 Balat

Balat was once home to the city's Sephardic Jewish and Armenian communities. Don't miss the 15th-century Ahrida Synagogue. *Map K1–2 • Bus 55T, 99A • Synagogue: Gevgili Sok. (0212) 523 74 07. Open by appointment*

### 7 Church of St Mary of the Mongols (Kanlı Kilise)

This beautiful church was built by Maria Palaeologina, a Byzantine princess who married a Mongol khan, and later became a nun. *Tekvir Cafer Mektebi Sok, Fener • Map L3 • (0212) 521 71 39 • Bus 55T, 99A • Open by appointment*

### 8 Palace of the Porphyrogenitus (Tekfur Sarayı)

Now just a shell, the Tekfur Palace once housed Byzantine emperors. *Şişhane Cad, Edirnekapı • Map J1 • Bus 87, 90, 126 • Groups only, by appointment with Haghia Sophia*

### 9 Eyüp Cemetery

A steep uphill walk leads past hundreds of Ottoman-era gravestones. There's a superb view of the Golden Horn. *Camii Kebir Sok • Map A4 • (0212) 564 73 68 • Bus 39, 55T, 99A*

### 10 Azap Kapı Mosque (Azap Kapı Camii)

Architect Sinan's 16th-century creation has an elegant marble *mihrab*. *Tersane Cad, Azapkapı • Map E3 • Bus 46H, 61B • Open prayer times only*

*Look out for the magnificent marble floor in the Church of the Pantocrator.*

**Price Categories**
For a typical meal of *meze* and main course for one without alcohol, and including taxes and extra charges.

| | |
|---|---|
| $ | under $7 |
| $$ | $7–13 |
| $$$ | $13–18 |
| $$$$ | $18–28 |
| $$$$$ | over $28 |

Pierre Loti Café

# TOP 10 Bars, Cafés and Restaurants

**1 Café du Levant, Sütlüce**
Part of the Rahmi Koç museum *(see p74)*, it serves stylish Gallic cuisine. *Hasköy Cad 27 • Map A4 • (0212) 369 66 07*

**2 Pierre Loti Café, Eyüp**
The interior of this hilltop café has traditional tiles, tea-making paraphernalia and exhibits relating to the novelist Pierre Loti *(see p74)*. Outside, the shady terrace offers fine views. *Gümüşsuyu Karyağdı Sok 5 • Map A4 • (0212) 581 26 96*

**3 Cibali Kapı Balıkçısı, Fener**
This traditional tavern serves fresh fish and wonderful *meze*. *Kadir Has Cad 5 • Map E3 • (0212) 533 28 46*

**4 Barba Giritli Balık Lokantası, Fener**
This two-storey restaurant offers excellent fish and *meze* such as *hamsi* (anchovies) and *ezme* (hot pepper dip). *Kadir Has Cad 3 • Map E3 • (0212) 533 18 66 • $$$$*

**5 Köfteci Arnavut, Balat**
Serving up *köfte* (meatballs) since 1947, this little eatery is the perfect place for a traditional Turkish lunch. The doors close when the *köfte* run out, usually by mid-afternoon. *Mürsel Paşa Cad 139, Köprübaşı • Map L2 • (0212) 531 66 52 • $*

**6 Ottoman Restaurant, Fener**
Ottoman *beğendi* – grilled lamb on aubergine cooked with cream and spices – comes with fine views. *Kadir Has Cad 11, Cibali • Map E3 • (0212) 631 75 67 • $$$$*

**7 Aziyade Restaurant, Pierre Loti**
This huge hotel restaurant serves traditional Ottoman dishes. *Turkuaz Boutique Hotel, İdris Köşkü Cad, Eyüp • Map A4 • (0212) 497 13 13 • $$$*

**8 Kömür, Fatih**
Locals flock to this simple café for delicious and ultra-cheap self-service dishes of Black Sea food. *Fevzipaşa Cad 18 • Map C4 • (0212) 631 40 04*

**9 Zeyrekhane Restaurant, Fatih**
Ottoman food is served on a terrace with fine views. Booking is advised. *İbadethane Arkası Sok 10, Zeyrek • Map D3 • (0212) 532 27 78 • Closed Mon • $$$*

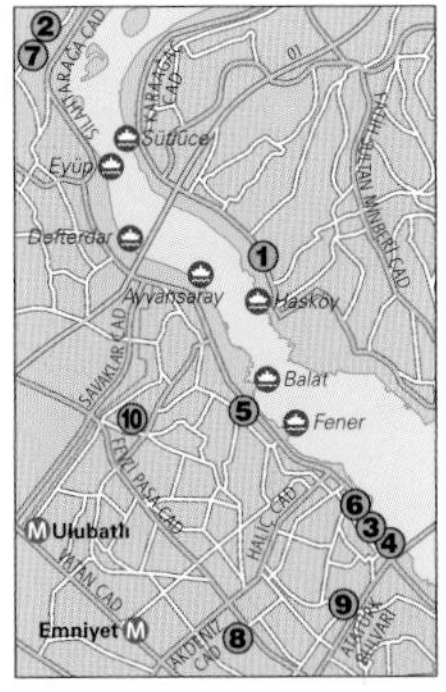


**10 Asitane Restaurant, Edirnekapı**
Dishes with delicate Ottoman flavours are served in a classy setting, with a summer courtyard. Reservations are recommended. *Kariye Oteli, Kariye Camii Sok 6 • Map C1 • (0212) 635 79 97 • $$$*

Traditional Ottoman dishes include minced chicken with nuts and spices; and lamb roasted with onions, dried fruit and nuts.

Left **Church of SS Peter and Paul** Right ***The Feast of Trotters*** **(artist unknown), Pera Museum**

# Beyoğlu

SET ON A STEEP HILL NORTH OF THE GOLDEN HORN, *facing the old town of Stamboul, is the "new town" of Beyoğlu, previously known as Pera – simply, "the other side". The area is hardly "new"; there has been a settlement here for 2,000 years. In the early Byzantine era, Pera was populated by Jewish merchants. In the late 13th century, Genoese merchants were given Galata as a reward for helping the Byzantines recapture the city from the Crusaders. In Ottoman times, European powers established embassies and trading centres, and Istanbul's commercial centre shifted here from the Grand Bazaar area. Today, Beyoğlu is the heart of modern European Istanbul, its streets (such as pedestrianized İstiklal Caddesi) lined with consulates, churches, stylish bars and all the latest shops.*

**Galata Tower and the waterfront of Beyoğlu**

## Top 10 Sights

1. Galata Tower
2. Pera Palace Hotel
3. İstiklal Caddesi
4. Galatasaray Baths
5. Military Museum
6. Taksim Square
7. Çukurcuma
8. Pera Museum
9. Church of SS Peter and Paul
10. French Street

## 1 Galata Tower (Galata Kulesi)

One of the city's most distinctive sights, the 70-m (230-ft) high tower was built in 1348 by the Genoese, the Byzantine Empire's greatest trading partners, as part of their fortification of Galata. Since then, the tower has survived several earthquakes, and been restored many times. There are 11 floors. A lift climbs to a viewing balcony, nightclub and restaurant on the top floor – the views of the Golden Horn and the city are fabulous. In the evenings, the restaurant hosts a dinner and cabaret with Turkish folk dance and belly dancing (see p84). *Büyük Hendek Sok • Map F2 • (0212) 293 81 80* • Viewing platform open *9am–7pm daily (dinner show from 8pm–1am) • Adm charge*

## 2 Pera Palace Hotel (Pera Palas Oteli)

Built in 1892 mainly for travellers on the Orient Express, the Pera Palace is Istanbul's most famous hotel. British thriller writer Agatha Christie stayed here often in the years 1924–33 and is said to have written *Murder on the Orient Express* in Room 411. Over the years, the hotel has also been frequented by figures such as Mata Hari, Leon Trotsky, Greta Garbo and Atatürk. In 1981, the Atatürk Museum Room was opened in his favourite room in the hotel, number 101. The exhibit displays many of his personal items. *Meşrutiyet Cad 98 • Map J5 • (0212) 222 80 90 • www.perapalace.com*

**Pera Palace Hotel, *circa* 1929**

## 3 İstiklal Caddesi

Packed with shoppers by day, Beyoğlu's main street (see p84) is an entertainment hub by night. It is pedestrianized, but you can hop on the tram, which runs the street's entire length. Be aware that the street numbers on İstiklal Caddesi are in the process of being changed. *Map J6–L4*

## 4 Galatasaray Baths (Tarihi Galatasaray Hamamı)

Wealthy İstanbullus come here to be sweated, scrubbed and scraped in one of the finest hamams in Istanbul, built by Beyazit II in 1481 and modernized without destroying the charm. The elegant decorations and fountains make it an aesthetic delight. Men and women bathe separately. *Turnacıbaşı Sok 24 (off İstiklal Cad) • Map K5 • (0212) 252 42 42 (men) & (0212) 249 43 42 (women) • Open 7am–10pm (men), 8am–9pm (women) daily • Adm charge*

**Entrance area, Galatasaray Baths**

Taksim Square

## 5 Military Museum (Askeri Müze)

Housed in the former military academy where Atatürk was educated, the museum contains thousands of exhibits telling the story of warfare from Ottoman times to World War II. Chain mail, bronze armour, swords and embroidered tents are displayed in separate halls. One room is devoted to Atatürk's career. A highlight is the performance each day by the Mehter Band, recreating the military music of the Janissaries, the elite Ottoman corps. *Vali Konağı Cad, Harbiye • Map B4 • (0212) 233 27 20 • 9am–5pm Wed–Sun (Mehter Band 3pm daily) • Adm charge*

Military helmet

### Military Marches

The Mehter music performed daily in the grounds of the Military Museum has been widely influential. Founded in the 14th century during the reign of Osman I, the Ottoman Janissary bands accompanied the army as it marched to war, intimidating the enemy through the sheer volume of their huge drums, cymbals and *zurnas* (traditional reed instruments). The rousing military style of Mehter music strongly influenced the compositions of Beethoven and Mozart, as well as the da Souza military marches played by today's brass bands.

## 6 Taksim Square (Taksim Meydanı)

The busy hub of modern Beyoğlu, Taksim Square was the end of the water supply line laid down by Mahmut I in 1732 – his original stone reservoir still stands at the square's southern end. On the western side of the square is the Monument of Independence, a patriotic sculpture of Atatürk and other revolutionary heroes erected in 1928. *Map L4*

## 7 Çukurcuma

The old quarter of Beyoğlu is today a centre for the furnishings and antiques trades. Its mansions and warehouses have been beautifully restored, and this is now a great place to browse for anything from antique cabinets to modern upholstery materials or 1960s comics. *Map K5*

## 8 Pera Museum (Pera Müzesi)

The old Bristol Hotel has been revived as the home of this museum and gallery, privately run by the Suna and İnan Kiraç Foundation set up by wealthy Turkish industrialists. The first two floors display the Kiraç family's collections of Kutahya tiles and ceramics and Anatolian weights and measures. The next floor has an intriguing collection, most of it by European artists, detailing life at the Ottoman Imperial court from the 17th century onwards. The top storeys are given over to temporary shows. *Meşrutiyet Cad 141 • Map J5 • (0212) 334 99 00 • Open 10am–7pm Tue–Sat, noon–6pm Sun • Adm charge*

## 9 Church of SS Peter and Paul (Sen Piyer Kilisesi)

When their original church was requisitioned as a mosque in the early 16th century, the Dominican brothers of Galata moved to this site, just below the Galata Tower. The church was built in the style of a basilica with four side altars. It also has a sky-blue cupola studded with gold stars over the choir. Mass is said here in Italian every morning. Ring the bell by the tiny door (accessed through the courtyard) to gain admittance. *Galata Kulesi Sok 44, Karaköy • Map F3 • (0212) 249 23 85 • Open 10:30am–noon Sun*

## 10 French Street (Fransız Sokağı)

This narrow street (officially called Cezayir Sokağı) was spruced up and now exudes a Gallic charm – hence its name-change. Several charming cafés, an art gallery and even century-old coal-gas street lamps recreate Beyoğlu's late-19th-century French atmosphere. Its restaurants serve fine French cuisine, and roof-top bars offer views aplenty. *Map K5*

French Street

## A Day in Beyoğlu

### Morning

Walk over the Galata Bridge and head up to the **Galata Tower**. Take the lift to the top to walk the perimeter balcony and enjoy the breathtaking morning view. Back at the bottom, refresh yourself at a traditional tea garden before taking a leisurely stroll up **Galip Dede Caddesi** to peer into the tiny music shops and have a go on a traditional Turkish instrument if the fancy takes you. Continue on towards **Tünel** and learn about the Whirling Dervishes at the **Mevlevi Monastery** *(see p82)*. For lunch, try a small street café on bohemian **Asmalı Mescit Sokağı**, or go Gallic on **French Street**.

### Afternoon

Walk up **İstiklal Caddesi** browsing the music shops, fashion stores and **Beyoğlu İş Merkezi** *(see p83)*, then visit the **Church of St Mary Draperis** and the **Church of Saint Anthony of Padua** *(see p82)*. Get to the **Military Museum** in time for the 3pm performance by the Mehter Band. Head to **Çukurcuma** via Taksim Square, stopping off for refreshment along the way if you need to catch your breath. After browsing the vast array of antique shops in Çukurcuma, relax at the **Galatasaray Baths**. Refreshed, wander past the **Galatasaray High School** and cut through to boisterous **Nevizade Sokağı** to choose a place to wine and dine. Fish is the speciality here – start with a few *meze* then try the catch of the day, washing it down with a glass of *rakı*.

Left **Nostalgic tram, İstiklal Caddesi** Right **Çiçek Pasajı**

# TOP 10 İstiklal Caddesi

### 1 Tünel

The 573-m (1,880-ft) Tünel is a funicular that runs up the steep slope from Galata Bridge to Beyoğlu. Built by the French in 1874, it is one of the world's oldest metros. *Map J6*

### 2 Christ Church

The centre of the Anglican community in Istanbul, this church was consecrated in 1868 as the Crimean Memorial Church, using English money and Maltese stone. *Serdar Ekrem Sok 83 • Map J6 • (0212) 251 56 16 • Free*

### 3 Mevlevi Monastery (Mevlevi Tekkesi)

This late 18th-century monastery belonged to a Sufi sect of Islamic mystics and is now the Whirling Dervish Museum (Mevlevihane Müzesi). Sufi Whirling Dervishes still dance here. *Galip Dede Cad 15 • Map J6 • (0212) 245 41 41 • Open 9am–4pm Wed–Mon • Adm charge; book in advance for dancing*

### 4 Royal Swedish Consulate

Built in 1757, this magnificent embassy was reconstructed after a fire in 1870. *İstiklal Cad 497 • Map J6 • (0212) 334 06 00 • Open for special events only*

### 5 Yapı Kredi Vedat Nedim Tör Müzesi

This small art gallery was set up by one of Turkey's largest banks. *İstiklal Cad 285 • Map J5 • (0212) 252 47 00 • Open 10am–6:45pm Mon–Fri, 10am–5:45pm Sat, 1–5:45pm Sun • Free*

### 6 Galatasaray High School (Galatasaray Lisesi)

Originally founded by Sultan Beyazıt II in 1481 to train Imperial pages, this is still Turkey's premier school. *İstiklal Cad • Map K5 • (0212) 249 11 00 • Closed to the public*

### 7 Balık Pazarı

A fabulous fish, fruit and veg market by day, by night these alleys are filled with cheap and lively restaurants. *Map J5*

### 8 Çiçek Pasajı

Housed in the Cité de Pera (1876), one of several ornate Victorian arcades along İstiklal, this former flower market is now an entertaining (if touristy) tavern quarter *(see p85)*. *Map K4*

### 9 Church of St Anthony of Padua

This red-brick Neo-Gothic building is the largest working Catholic church in the city. It was built in 1912 by Istanbul-born Italian architect Giulio Mongeri. *İstiklal Cad 171 • Map J5 • (0212) 244 09 35 • Open 8am–7:30pm daily (closed 12:30–3pm Sun) • Free*

### 10 Nostalgic Tram

The horse-drawn tram service that rumbled along İstiklal Caddesi in the 19th century was electrified in 1914 (the horses were taken off to war). The service closed in 1961, but was revived in 1990. Its cheery red carriages have become an icon of Beyoğlu. Buy tickets at either end of the line. *Map J5–L4*

Left **Music shop on Galip Dede Caddesi** Right **Ali Muhiddin Hacı Bekir**

# Top 10 Shopping

**1 Aznavur Pasajı**
This Italian-style arcade has been on İstiklal Caddesi since 1883. You can buy a range of handmade goods here, including jewellery, clothes and souvenirs, on any of the nine floors. *İstiklal Cad 108, Galatasaray Meydanı • Map K5*

**2 Galip Dede Caddesi**
Musical instruments, such as the traditional *oud*, handmade violins and second-hand accordions, are sold at a string of specialist music shops in this small street. *Tünel • Map J6*

**3 Çukurcuma**
These streets between Cihangir and Galatasaray are the best spot for antique-hunting. *Map K5*

**4 Avrupa Pasajı**
The 22 shops in this quiet, attractive old arcade carry a fine selection of jewellery, ceramics and other traditional Turkish crafts. There are also quirkier souvenirs such as old prints and maps. *Meşrutiyet Cad 16 • Map J5*

**5 Beyoğlu İş Merkezi**
A haven for bargain-hunters, the three-storey Beyoğlu İş Merkezi is filled with tiny shops selling mainly high-street fashion labels. Many of the products here are slight seconds or surplus, hence the rock-bottom prices. A tailor's shop in the basement can make alterations on the same day. *İstiklal Cad 187 • Map J5*

**6 Mavi Jeans**
Jeans made from organic cotton and hip T-shirts are among the stylish offerings available from one of Turkey's most popular fashion brands. *İstiklal Cad 123 • Map K5*

**7 Koton**
You'll find both men's and women's fashions at this reasonably priced Turkish chain store. Designs are updated regularly and include party- and daywear. *İstiklal Cad 54 in Demirören AVM • Map K4*

**8 Paşabahçe**
The flagship showroom of one of the world's largest glass manufacturers sells affordable modern and traditional glassware, all made in Turkey. *İstiklal Cad 150 • Map J5*

**9 Robinson Crusoe**
Pick up the latest Elif Safak or Orhan Pamuk novel – or discover a favourite Turkish writer of your own – at this high-ceilinged temple to the written word. Also carries a good selection of English-language magazines. *İstiklal Cad 195A • Map J5*

**10 Ali Muhiddin Hacı Bekir**
*The* place for *lokum* (Turkish Delight), this is the Beyoğlu branch of the confectioners who invented the stuff in 1777. Other tasty treats include *akide* (colourful boiled sweets), *helva*, *baklava* and marzipan. *İstiklal Cad 83A • Map K4*

Left **Nardis Jazz Club** Centre **Al Jamal** Right **Riddim**

# TOP 10 Nightlife

### 1 Nardis Jazz Club
There's live music every night. Find a table near the stage and choose from the menu of salads and pasta. *Kuledibi Sok 14 • Map F3 • (0212) 244 63 27*

### 2 Babylon
Babylon is indisputably the city's best venue for live music of every kind. *Şeyhbender Sok 3 • Map J6 • (0212) 292 73 68*

### 3 Al Jamal
Stretch out on the chandelier-lit sofa seating and splash out for quality belly dancing (including male dancers in drag) and fine food. Al Jamal attracts high-rolling Turks rather than the usual tourists, and offers a more authentic experience. *Taşkişla Cad 13, Maçka • Map H1 • (0212) 296 09 69*

### 4 Indigo
With a resident DJ and live guest acts, this dimly lit, super-hip club is for serious lovers of electronic music. *İstiklal Cad, Akarsu Sok 1–5 • Map J5 • (0212) 244 85 67*

### 5 Süheyla
Süheyla is one of the best places to hear *fasıl* – the music of the *meyhanes (see p110)*, part Turkish classical, part wild Gypsy, always enthusiastically and noisily greeted by the sing-along crowd. The set menu includes unlimited *rakı*. *Kalyoncu Kulluk Cad 19 (behind Balık Pazarı) • Map J5 • (0212) 251 83 47*

### 6 Riddim
Resident DJs and occasional live acts serve up a mix of R&B, reggae, hip-hop, Latin and world music in this slick but tourist-friendly club. *Sıraselviler Cad 35/1 • Map L4 • (0212) 251 27 23*

### 7 Garajlstanbul
Tucked away on a Beyoğlu backstreet, this club offers an adventurous program of theatre performances, live bands and other cultural events. *Kaymakam Reşat Bey Sok 11A, off Yeni Çarşi Cad • Map K5 • (0212) 244 44 99*

### 8 360
The beautiful people flock to this rooftop terrace. The club offers lounge music with dinner, and a resident DJ for a funkier dance sound after midnight. The 360° views are superb. *İstikal Cad 311 • Map J5 • (0212) 251 10 42*

### 9 Peyote
This popular local venue for alternative and world-music bands draws a hip, young crowd with its low prices and up-and-coming acts. *Kameriye Sok 4, off Hamalbaşi Cad • Map J4 • (0212) 251 43 98*

### 10 Salon İKSV
An intimate venue for classical, jazz, world music and other concerts, as well as dance performances and theatre. There are also interesting modern adaptations of traditional dramas. *Sadi Konuralp Cad 5, off Refik Saydam Cad • Map J6 • (0212) 334 07 00*

Leb-i-Derya

**Price Categories**

For a typical meal of *meze* and main course for one without alcohol, and including taxes and extra charges.

| | |
|---|---|
| $ | under $7 |
| $$ | $7–13 |
| $$$ | $13–18 |
| $$$$ | $18–28 |
| $$$$$ | over $28 |

# Top 10 Bars, Cafés and Restaurants

**1 Nevizade Sokak**
Several little fish restaurants on one tiny street serve the catch of the day, washed down with *rakı*. *Map K4 • $$$*

**2 Ara Café**
There's an intellectual, artistic vibe at this café serving fresh, light food (but no alcohol). It is decorated with the work of Turkey's most famous photographer, Ara Güler. *Tosbağa Sok 8, off Yeni Çarşi Cad • Map J5 • (0212) 245 41 05 • $$$*

**3 Refik**
A true *meyhane* with *meze*, free-flowing wine and a bohemian clientele, Refik is stuck in the past and all the better for it. *Sofyali Sok 10–12 • Map J6 • (0212) 243 28 34 • $$*

**4 Galata House**
This is a true original – a restaurant in a converted British jail. It serves delicious Russian-Georgian-Turkish food. *Galata Kulesi Sok 15 • Map F2 • (0212) 245 18 61 • Closed Mon • $$$*

**5 Yakup 2**
The Yakup 2 has a smoky, alcohol-rich atmosphere popular with large groups. The food is excellent, with a wide choice of *meze*, salads and grills. *Asmalımescit Sok 21 • Map J6 • (0212) 249 29 25 • $$*

**6 Hala Mantı**
Hearty Turkish food such as *mantı*, a kind of pasta, are served at this popular eatery. *Büyükparmakkapı, Çukurlu Ceşme Sok 14/A • Map L4 • (0212) 293 75 31 • $*

**7 Leb-i-Derya**
Start with a cocktail, then sample their speciality, the 40-spiced *steak Mahmudiye*. Come early if you want to eat on the tiny roof terrace. Reservations are essential at weekends. *Kumbaracı Yokuşu 57/6 • Map J6 • (0212) 293 49 89 • $$$*

**8 Zencefil**
Light, tasty vegetarian food in European style is on offer at this lovely little café-restaurant with a summer garden. *Kurabiye Sok 8–10 • Map K4 • (0212) 243 82 34 • $*

**9 Pano Şarap Evi**
Beer and wine flow freely at this popular historic backstreet wine house. *Hamalbaşı Cad 12/B • Map J4 • (0212) 292 66 64*

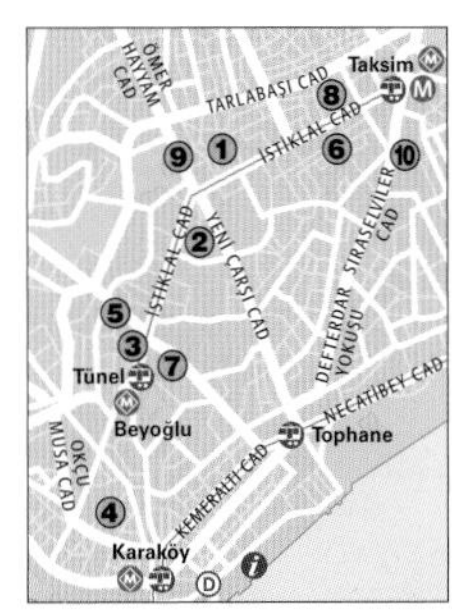


**10 Changa**
This chic modern restaurant in an Art-Nouveau building serves fabulous Pacific-fusion cuisine. An inset glass floor allows guests to watch the chefs below. *Sıraselviler Cad 47 • Map L5 • (0212) 249 13 48 • Closed Sun • $$$$$*

Recommend your favourite bar on traveldk.com

Left **Istanbul Museum of Modern Art** Right **View across the Bosphorus to the Asian shore**

# The Bosphorus

THE BOSPHORUS IS ONE OF THE WORLD'S *busiest waterways, part of the only shipping lane from the Black Sea to the Mediterranean. Just 32 km (20 miles) long and varying in width from 3 km (about 2 miles) to 672 m (2,205 ft), it connects the Black Sea to the Sea of Marmara, dividing Europe from Asia. The straits are governed by international maritime law, so Turkey has authority only over vessels flying a Turkish flag. Navigation can be difficult, since the mixture of fresh water from the Black Sea and salt water from the Sea of Marmara creates complex cross-currents. All of this is fascinating, but to most of us, what really counts is the beauty of the waterway and the historic buildings that line its shores.*

**Imposing walls and bastions of the Fortress of Europe**

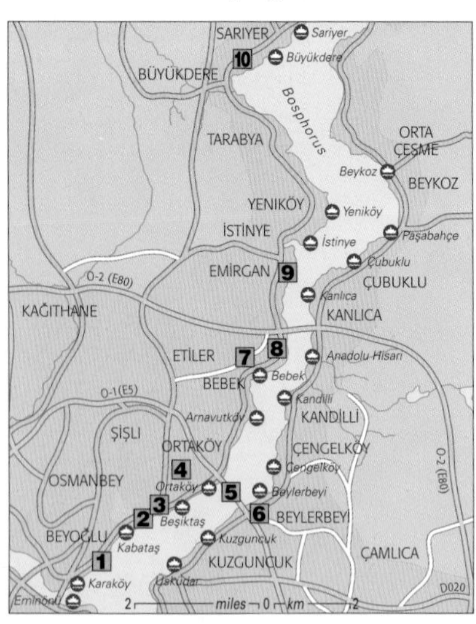


## Top 10 Sights

1. Istanbul Museum of Modern Art
2. Dolmabahçe Palace
3. Naval Museum
4. Yıldız Palace
5. Bosphorus Bridge
6. Beylerbeyi Palace
7. Aşiyan Museum
8. Fortress of Europe
9. Sakıp Sabancı Museum
10. Sadberk Hanım Museum



Preceding pages **İznik tiles on one of the interior walls of the Blue Mosque**

## 1 Istanbul Museum of Modern Art (İstanbul Modern Sanat Müzesi)

This cutting-edge gallery's small permanent collection of modern Turkish painting, sculpture and photography is augmented by touring exhibitions, video and audio installations, and an art-house cinema. *Meclis-i Mebusan Cad, Karaköy • Map G2 • (0212) 334 73 00 • www.istanbulmodern.org • Open 10am–6pm Tue–Sun (to 8pm Thu) • Adm charge*

**Alabaster bathroom, Dolmabahçe Palace**

## 2 Dolmabahçe Palace (Dolmabahçe Sarayı)

In 1853, Sultan Abdül Mecit removed his entire family and government from the Topkapı to this European-style palace at Beşiktaş on the Bosphorus shore *(see pp26–7)*.

## 3 Naval Museum (Deniz Müzesi)

Ottoman Turkey's great maritime history is celebrated in this vividly accessible museum, which consists of two buildings beside the ferry landing in Beşiktaş. In the first block are lavishly adorned Imperial caïques – high-prowed barges that were used for ferrying the royal family along the Bosphorus. The largest, built for Sultan Mehmet IV in 1648, was 40 m (130 ft) long and required 144 *bostancıs* (oarsmen) to row it. The other building holds a selection of figureheads, captured standards, weaponry, paintings and engravings – along with furnishings from Atatürk's private yacht, the *Savarona*. *Hayrettin Paşa İskelesi Sok, Beşiktaş • Map C5 • (0212) 327 43 45 • Tram Kabataş then 5-min walk • Open 9am–5pm Wed–Sun • Adm charge*

**Rowing boat used by Atatürk, Naval Museum**

## 4 Yıldız Palace (Yıldız Sarayı)

Much of this rambling palace was built by Sultan Abdül Hamit II (ruled 1876–1909), a highly skilled carpenter whose former workshop now houses the Yıldız Palace Museum. The park and its pavilions are also open to the public. In the grounds is the Imperial Porcelain Factory, now mass-producing china where once they manufactured fine porcelain. *Yıldız Cad, Beşiktaş • Map C4 • (0212) 258 30 81 • Palace open 9:30am–4:30pm Wed–Mon; park open 10am–4pm daily (to 5:30pm in winter) • Adm charge*

**Şale Pavilion, Yıldız Palace Park**

Marble fountain in an atrium of Beylerbeyi Palace

### 5 Bosphorus Bridge (Boğaziçi Köprüsü)

In 1973, to mark the 50th anniversary of the establishment of the Republic of Turkey, this soaring creation, linking Europe and Asia across the Bosphorus straits, was officially opened. At 1,560 m (5,120 ft) long, it is the world's sixth-longest suspension bridge. Pedestrians are not allowed onto the bridge, so if you want plenty of time to admire the view, cross at rush hour when the heavy traffic routinely becomes gridlocked. *Map C4*

### 6 Beylerbeyi Palace (Beylerbeyi Sarayı)

This small, frivolously ornate powder-puff of a palace was built in 1860–65 by Sultan Abdül Aziz as a summer retreat. It was here that Sultan Abdül Hamit II lived out his days in captivity after he was deposed in 1909. You will either be charmed or overwhelmed by the incredible detailing of architect Sarkis Balyan's Oriental Rococo style. Look for the inlaid stairs in the Fountain Room, the hand-decorated doorknobs, the Bohemian crystal chandeliers, the Hereke carpets and the walnut-and-rosewood furniture made by Abdül Hamit himself *(see also p89)*. *Çayırbaşı Cad (next to Bosphorus Bridge) • Map C5 • (0216) 321 93 20 • Bus 15 from Üsküdar • Open 9am–5pm (to 4pm Oct–Apr) Tue, Wed, Fri–Sun (guided tours only) • Adm charge*

#### Princely Paranoia

Terrified both of plots to seize his throne and of seaborne attack by foreign warships on Dolmabahçe Palace, Sultan Abdül Hamit II (ruled 1876–1909) removed himself from the Dolmabahçe to live at the much smaller Yıldız Palace *(see p89)*, the core of which – the State Apartments (Büyük Mabeyn) – dates to the reign of Sultan Selim III (ruled 1789–1807). Abdül Hamit built a sprawling complex of pavilions and villas in the palace grounds, and he supposedly never spent two nights in the same bed. He was overthrown in April 1909.

### 7 Aşiyan Museum (Aşiyan Müzesi)

The poet and utopian philosopher Tevfik Fikret (1867–1915), founder of the Edebiyat-i Cedid (New Literature) movement, built this wooden mansion, now on the campus of Boğaziçi University, in 1906. It recalls the movement with the personal belongings and photos of the members. *Aşiyan Yolu, Bebek • Map U4 • (0212) 263 69 82 • Open 9am–4:30pm Tue, Wed, Fri, Sat*

### 8 Fortress of Europe (Rumeli Hisarı)

In 1452, as he prepared for his final attack on Constantinople, Mehmet II built this vast fortress at the narrowest point of the Bosphorus, opposite the earlier Fortress of Asia (Anadolu Hisarı) *(see p92)*, to cut the flow of supplies reaching the city. The castle's three main towers are surrounded by a huge curtain wall with 13 bastions. The main tower later became a prison. Following restoration in 1953, the fortress is now a venue for open-air theatre. *Yahya Kemal Cad • Map U4 • (0212) 263 53 05 • Open 9am–4:30pm Thu–Tue • Adm charge*

## 9 Sakıp Sabancı Museum (Sakıp Sabancı Müzesi)

The summer residence of the Sabancı family of industrialists from 1951 to 1999, the Atlı Köşk (Horse Mansion) is now a museum set in stunning gardens that overlook the Bosphorus. The exhibits include calligraphy of the Ottoman era, and paintings by leading 19th- and 20th-century Turkish artists. The modern extension is a well-designed art gallery housing major touring exhibitions. *Sakıp Sabancı Cad 22, Emirgan • Map U3 • (0212) 277 22 00 • Open 10am–6pm Tue–Sun (to 10pm Wed) • Adm charge*

## 10 Sadberk Hanım Museum (Sadberk Hanım Müzesi)

A must-see collection includes Turkish embroidery as well as Anatolian figurines, Assyrian cuneiform trade tablets, Hittite coins, and gold jewellery. *Piyasa Cad 25–9, Büyükdere • Map U2 • (0212) 242 38 13 • www.sadberkhanimmuzesi.org.tr • Open 10am–5pm Thu–Tue • Adm charge*

**Sadberk Hanım Museum**

## A Walk Through Karaköy

### Morning

Start your day at the fish market off **Karaköy Square**. From here, Haraççı Ali Sok brings you to the **Jewish Museum** in the 17th-century Zülfaris synagogue. Turn left along **Voyvoda Caddesi**, named for Vlad the Impaler whose decapitated head (it is said) was displayed here. This was the old banking centre and has some fine old buildings. The **Kamondo Steps** lead towards the Galata Tower. Walk back down along Karaköy Caddesi and turn right to visit **Yeraltı Camii**, a 19th-century mansion hiding a mosque and the ruins of a Byzantine Castle.

### Afternoon

Back in Karaköy Square, turn left onto **Rihtim Caddesi**. The **Güllüoğlu** *baklava* shop here is the finest in Turkey, with pastries sold by the kilo; the **Galata Rihtim Köftecisi** nearby offers a healthier option for lunch. Follow the road round between two fine small mosques, the **Nusretiye Mosque** (on the right), built by Kirkor Balyan in the 1820s, and the **Kılıç Ali Paşa Mosque**, built by Sinan in 1580 and named after a famous admiral in Süleyman I's navy. Turn right onto the main road and, just after the Mimar Sinan University building, turn right again. Follow the signs through the old docks area to **Istanbul Modern** *(see p89)* where you can watch the sunset with a cocktail in the chic café-bar over-looking the Bosphorus. Then take the metro to Kabataş and the funicular up the hill to Taksim, for dinner and a view at **Changa** *(see p85)*.

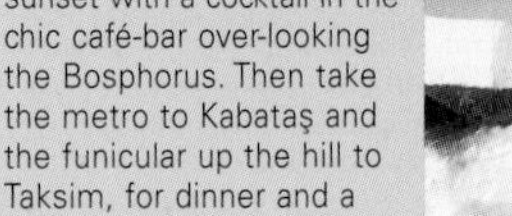



For more on Bosphorus cruises **See pp28–9**

Left **Fortress of Asia** Centre **Çırağan Palace Gateway** Right **Ortaköy**

# TOP 10 Best of the Rest

**1 Museum of Painting and Sculpture (Resim ve Heykel Müzesi)**
Fine art from the 19th and 20th centuries is displayed in the Crown Princes' Suite at Dolmabahçe Palace. *Hayrettin Paşa Iskelesi Sok, Beşiktaş • Map C5 • (0212) 261 42 98 • Bus 25E, 28, 40, 56 • Open 10am–4:30pm Tue–Sat • Free*

**2 Çırağan Palace (Çırağan Sarayı)**
Sultan Abdül Aziz spent a fortune on this confection of a palace, built in 1874, before pronouncing it damp and moving out. It is now a luxury hotel. *Çırağan Cad 32, Beşiktaş • Map C5 • (0212) 258 33 77 • www.ciragan-palace.com • Bus 25E, 40*

**3 Ortaköy**
This pretty village beside the Bosphorus Bridge has many waterfront cafés, restaurants and clubs, and a weekend craft market. *Map C5 • Bus 25E, 40*

**4 Automobile Museum (SAV Otomobil Müzesi)**
Here you will find Turkey's largest collection of antique cars. *104 Nato Yolu, Bosna Bulvarı, Çengelköy (Asian side) • Map U4 • (0216) 329 50 30 • Open Tue–Sun • Adm charge*

**5 Arnavutköy**
Once noted for its strawberries, the village of Arnavutköy is now better known for the charming *yalıs* (wooden mansions) that line its waterfront. *Map U4 • Ferry or road*

**6 Küçüksu Palace (Küçüksu Kasrı)**
Beykoz, with two rivers known to the Ottomans as the "Sweet Waters of Asia", was a playground for the Imperial court. This palace was built as a hunting lodge in 1857 for Abdül Mecit. *Küçüksu Cad, Beykoz (Asian side) • Map V3 • (0216) 332 33 03 • Bus 15 from Üsküdar • Open 9:30am–4pm Tue, Wed, Fri–Sun • Adm charge*

**7 Fortress of Asia (Anadolu Hisarı)**
Built by Beyazit I in 1391, this fortress on the Asian Side is a smaller counterpart to the Fortress of Europe, added by Mehmet II in 1452, directly across the Bosphorus *(see p90)*. *Map U4 • Boat or road to Kanlıca • Call (0212) 263 53 05 to visit*

**8 Emirgan Park (Emirgan Parkı)**
This attractive park with botanic planting is the venue for the Tulip Festival each April. *Emirgan Sahil Yolu • Map U3 • (0212) 277 57 82 • Bus 25E, 40 • Open 7am–10:30pm daily*

**9 Tarabya**
First settled by wealthy Greeks in the 18th century, the village of Tarabya has some fine fish restaurants. *Map U2 • Ferry or road*

**10 Anadolu Kavağı**
This is the last stop for the Bosphorus ferry. Climb the hill to the Genoese Castle, a ruined 14th-century Byzantine fortress. *Map V2 • Asian side; ferry or road*

Kordon

**Price Categories**

| For a typical meal of *meze* and main course for one without alcohol, and including taxes and extra charges. | | |
|---|---|---|
| | $ | under $7 |
| | $$ | $7–13 |
| | $$$ | $13–18 |
| | $$$$ | $18–28 |
| | $$$$$ | over $28 |

# Top 10 Bars, Cafés and Restaurants

**1 Amerikan Pasajı**
Choose from among the *nargile* cafés in this alley. Some stay open all night and allow you to bring in food from the stalls nearby. *Tophane-Karaköy • Map F3*

**2 Laledan, Beşiktaş**
Part of the luxurious Çırağan Palace Hotel Kempinski, the Laledan serves great brunches in a fairytale setting. *Çırağan Cad, Beşiktaş • Map C5 • (0212) 258 33 77 • $$$$$*

**3 Vogue**
Booking is essential at this chic restaurant serving sushi and fusion cuisine, situated on the 13th floor of a tower block. *Spor Cad 48, BJK Plaza A, Blok 13, Beşiktaş • Map C5 • (0212) 227 25 45 • $$$$*

**4 Feriye Lokantası**
Picturesquely situated on the Ortaköy waterfront, the Feriye serves delicious Ottoman dishes including charcoal-grilled lamb. Book ahead. *Çırağan Cad 40, Ortaköy • Map U4 • (0212) 227 22 16/7 • $$$$*

**5 The House Café**
This café serves unusual pizzas (like pear, roquefort and honey), together with seafood, and brunch staples. Its waterfront decking is a draw in summer, when office workers come for a post-work drink and young people for after-dinner partying. *Yıldız Mahallesi, Salhane Sok 1, Ortaköy • Map U4 • (0212) 227 26 99 • Reservations recommended for brunch*

**6 Angelique**
On the first-floor waterfront terrace is the upmarket Da Mario Italian restaurant (summer only), while the second and third floors serve international cuisine and become a nightclub after the dishes are cleared away. *Muallim Naci Cad, Salhane Sok 5, Ortaköy • Map U4 • (0212) 327 28 44/5 • $$$$*

**7 Istanbul Jazz Center**
A major venue during the annual jazz festival, this lively place serves food on the terrace and inside. Live music every night except Sunday. *Çırağan Caddasi Salhane Sok 10, Ortaköy • Map U4 • (0212) 327 50 50*

**8 Kordon**
This chic seafood restaurant offers stunning views and mouthwatering food. *Kuleli Cad 51, Çengelköy (Asian side) • Map U4 • (0216) 321 04 73 • $$$$*

**9 Reina**
Dance to European club sounds at this unashamedly pretentious nightspot. *Muallim Naci Cad 44, Ortaköy • Map U4 • (0212) 259 59 19 • Adm charge Fri, Sat; free at other times*

**10 Abracadabra**
Overlooking the Bosphorous, this restaurant has an artistic vibe. Innovative dishes, such as salmon tartar with bulgar, slow-cooked duck and curried banana mousse, are served here. *Arnavutköy Cad 50 • Map U4 • (0212) 358 60 87 • $$$$*

*Recommend your favourite restaurant on traveldk.com*

Left **Leander's Tower** Right **Doll's house, Istanbul Toy Museum**

# Asian Istanbul

ASIAN ISTANBUL IS PREDOMINANTLY RESIDENTIAL, *but this little-visited part of the city has many hidden treasures. Around Üsküdar you can see several of Sinan's mosques, take in the jaw-dropping views from the top of Büyük Çamlıca and visit the Florence Nightingale Museum in the Selimiye army barracks. You can wander the markets in Kadıköy and drop into the cafés along Bağdat Caddesi. The pretty harbour at Moda attracts day-trippers, while passengers arrive and depart in droves at castle-like Haydarpaşa Station. Frequent ferries from Eminönü make it an easy hop between continents.*

**Tomb of the warrior Karacaahmet**

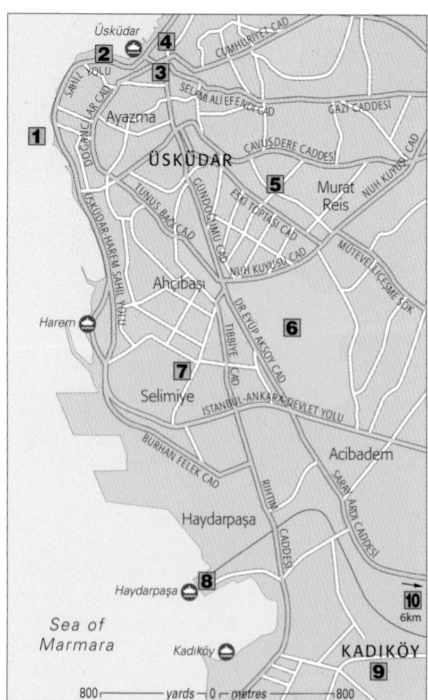


## Top 10 Sights

1. Leander's Tower
2. Şemsi Paşa Mosque
3. Yeni Valide Mosque
4. İskele Mosque
5. Atik Valide Mosque
6. Karaca Ahmet Cemetery
7. Florence Nightingale Museum
8. Haydarpaşa Station
9. Kadıköy
10. Istanbul Toy Museum

*If you are telephoning anyone on the Asian side from the European side, don't forget to add the code: 0216.*

### 1 Leander's Tower (Kız Kulesi)

According to Greek myth, Leander drowned while trying to swim the Dardanelles from his home town of Abydos on the Asian side to meet his lover Hero, a priestess in Sestos on the other shore. He is commemorated in the English name for this 18th-century tower on an islet offshore from Üsküdar. Its Turkish name means "Maiden's Tower", in reference to a legendary Byzantine princess who was told that she would die of snakebite and was locked up on the island for her own protection, only for a snake to arrive in a basket of figs. In its time, the tower has served as a quarantine centre and a customs office; nowadays it houses a restaurant. It had a cameo role in the 1999 James Bond film *The World Is Not Enough.* *Map W3 • (0216) 342 47 47 • Tower open 12:30–6:30pm Mon–Fri, 9:15am–6:30pm Sat & Sun; restaurant open to 1am*

Ablutions fountain, İskele Mosque

### 2 Şemsi Paşa Mosque (Şemsi Paşa Camii)

Legend has it that birds will not land on or dirty this mosque out of respect for its beauty and the reputation of its architect. It is one of Mimar Sinan's last works *(see p21)*, built in 1580 for Şemsi Ahmet Paşa, Grand Vizier to Süleyman I. Made of white stone, it is very modest in size and sits in a picturesque location among the waterfront fish restaurants. *Sahil Yolu • Map W2 • Ferry Üsküdar • Open daily • Free*

### 3 Yeni Valide Mosque (Yeni Valide Camii)

This imposing mosque was built in 1710 by Ahmet III for his mother, Gülnuş Emetullah. *Hakimiyeti Milliye Cad • Map X2 • Ferry Üsküdar • Open daily*

### 4 İskele Mosque (İskele Camii)

This beautiful mosque is also known as the Mihrimah Mosque – it was a present, built in 1547–8, from Süleyman I to his favourite daughter, Mihrimah. Its raised portico offers fine views down to the main square. *Hakimiyeti Milliye Cad • Map X2 • (0216) 321 93 20 • Ferry Üsküdar • Open daily (closed at prayer times) • Free*

### 5 Atik Valide Mosque (Atik Valide Camii)

Set on a hill, the huge complex of the Old Mosque of the Sultan's Mother was completed in 1583 for Nur Banu Valide Sultan, the Venetian-born Jewish wife of Selim II. Sinan's finest work, it retains many glorious details. *Çinili Cami Sok • Map Y3 • Bus 12C from Üsküdar • Open prayer times only*

Şemsi Paşa Mosque, Üsküdar

### 6 Karaca Ahmet Cemetery (Karacaahmet Mezarlığı)

The largest graveyard in Turkey, this Muslim cemetery was founded in the 14th century. It is named after the warrior Karacaahmet, whose highly venerated tomb is here. It is a pleasant place in which to stroll among the old cypresses and ancient, symbolic tombstones. *Nuh Kuyusu Cad, Selimiye • Map Y5 • Bus 12 • Open 9:30am–5:30pm; tomb open 9:30am–4:30pm daily*

### 7 Florence Nightingale Museum

In the northwest tower of the Selimiye Barracks is a moving tribute to the formidable Englishwoman Florence Nightingale (1820–1910), who in 1854 gathered a group of 38 women and set up a hospital in Istanbul to nurse thousands of Turkish and allied soldiers wounded during the Crimean War – inventing modern nursing practice along the way. The museum contains her photographs and medallions, gifts from Sultan Abdül Mecit, and the lamp from which she got her nickname, "the Lady of the Lamp". The vast, forbidding barracks in which the museum is situated were begun in 1828 by Mahmut II to replace an earlier military building constucted by Selim III. *Selimiye Kışlası, Çeşme-i-Kebir Cad • Map X5 • (0216) 556 81 66 • Ferry to Harem • Open 9am–5pm Mon–Fri • Free • Visitors should fax (0216) 310 79 29 requesting permission to visit, at least 2 days in advance, giving names, nationalities, passport details and contact number*

**Bust of Florence Nightingale**

#### Nursing Pioneers

Florence Nightingale is justly famous for her pioneering wartime work. By contrast, Mary Seacole, born in Jamaica in 1805, is now a largely forgotten heroine. Seacole had nursed family members since her childhood, and at the onset of the Crimean War she decided to offer her services to England. Told that there were no vacancies for nurses, she headed straight for the battlefield, and nursed soldiers injured on the front line. After the war, she was fêted by British high society and published her autobiography, but her contribution has never been properly acknowledged.

### 8 Haydarpaşa Station

Haydarpaşa Station is the largest station in Turkey and the most westerly train stop in Asia. It was completed in 1908 by German architects Otto Ritter and Helmuth Cuno, a gift from the German government of Kaiser Wilhelm II. These days, the station is the departure point for travellers heading further into Anatolia or across to Syria; trains to Europe depart from Sirkeci Station *(see p58)*. However, a tunnel beneath the Bosphorus is under construction that will link the two continents and two stations. *Haydarpaşa İstasyon Cad • Map C6 • (0216) 336 04 75 • Ferry to Haydarpaşa or Kadıköy*

**Haydarpaşa Station**

Food shopping in the Old Bazaar, Kadıköy

## 9 Kadıköy

Kadıköy, first settled as long ago as the Neolithic era, was the site of the Greek colony of Chalcedon, founded in 676 BC, nine years before the establishment of Byzantion *(see p56)*. However, Chalcedon proved to more be vulnerable to invaders than Byzantion, and it failed to flourish. Today, Kadıköy is a popular and attractive shopping area, but it has maintained its cosy, neighbourhood feel. The lively market area by the docks has fresh fruit and vegetables galore and is a good place to stock up on provisions. Fenerbahçe – one of Turkey's top football clubs – has its grounds, Şükrü Saraçoğlu Stadium, close by, so watch out for traffic jams on match days. A nostalgic tram rumbles through the area down to fashionable Moda *(see p98)*, where you can enjoy a pleasant seafront stroll. *Map C6 • Frequent ferries from Eminönü*

## 10 Istanbul Toy Museum (İstanbul Oyuncak Müzesi)

Highlights of this collection of toys and miniatures from around the world include a toymaker's shop, a French miniature violin from 1817, and a US doll from the 1820s. *Ömerpaşa Cad, Dr Zeki Zeren Sok 17, Göztepe • Map U5 • (0216) 359 45 50/1 • Open 9:30am–6pm Tue–Sun • Adm charge • www.istanbuloyuncakmuzesi.com*

## A Day in Asia

### Morning

Take an early ferry from Eminönü to **Üsküdar** and, from there, sail to the legend-steeped **Leander's Tower.** The top of the tower is a great place to have a mid-morning snack. Back on the Asian shore, explore the mosques of Üsküdar, then make your way south to the majestic **Haydarpaşa Station**, and the **Selimiye Army Barracks** (having faxed ahead as they are still a military headquarters), the site of the Crimean-War-era military hospital and the fascinating **Florence Nightingale Museum**. Afterwards, you may wish to take a contemplative walk among the sombre memorials of the **British Crimean Cemetery** *(see p98)* and the peaceful sea of tombstones in the **Karaca Ahmet Cemetery**, with its estimated one million inhabitants.

### Afternoon

If, after this, you feel like a change of mood, head south into **Kadıköy** with its bustling shops and markets. Stop for lunch in one of the lively bars and cafés of **Kadife Sokak** (Bar Street) *(see p99)*, many of which have live music. Afterwards, catch the tram down to **Moda** *(see p98)* for a stroll along the seafront promenade with an ice cream or, more expensively, take your credit card for a spin through the designer stores along **Bağdat Caddesi** *(see p98)*. Have an early supper at trendy **Zanzibar** *(see p98)* on the quay at Caddebostan before taking a taxi to the ferry terminus at Kadıköy and catching an evening ferry back across to the European side.

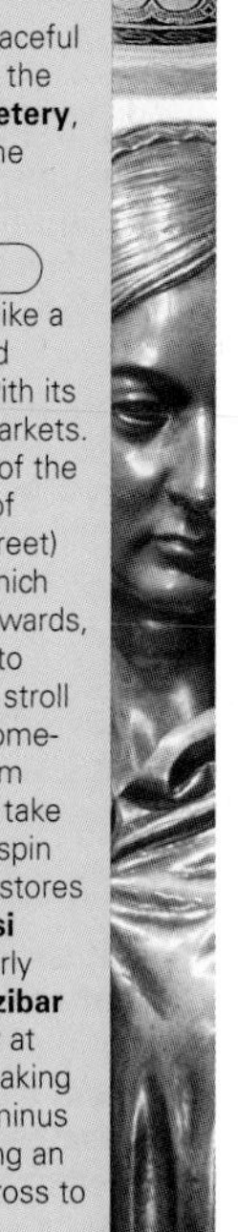

*If you're planning to have dinner in Kadıköy then return by ferry to the European side, note that the last ferry departs at 11pm.*

Left **View of the city from Büyük Çamlıca** Right **Waterfront at Moda**

# Top 10 Best of the Rest

### 1 İskele Meydanı

Üsküdar's lively main square (officially named – but never called – Demokrasi Meydanı) contains the Yeni Valide and İskele mosques and the Baroque, four-sided Fountain of Ahmet III, built in 1728. *Map X2 • Ferry to Üsküdar*

### 2 Mimar Sinan Bazaar (Mimar Sinan Çarşısı)

This former bathhouse, built by Sinan in 1574–83 *(see p21)* was converted into a bazaar in 1962. *Hakimiyet-i Milliye Cad, Üsküdar • Map X2 • Ferry to Üsküdar*

### 3 Rumi Mehmet Paşa Mosque (Rumi Mehmet Paşa Camii)

Commissioned by Grand Vizier Rumi Mehmet Paşa and finished in 1471, this is one of Istanbul's oldest surviving mosques. *Rumi Mehmet Paşa Mah, Eşref Sok, Üsküdar • Map W2 • Ferry to Üsküdar*

### 4 Tiled Mosque (Çinili Cami)

Don't miss the glorious explosion of İznik tiles inside this mosque, built in 1640. *Çinili Hamam Sok 1, Üsküdar • Map Y3 • Ferry Üsküdar, then 20 mins walk • Open prayer times only*

### 5 British Crimean War Cemetery

Most of the 6,000 Crimean War soldiers in this cemetery died of cholera rather than in battle. The War Memorial was erected in 1857. *Off Burhan Felek Cad • Map X6 • Ferry Harem then 15 mins walk*

### 6 Büyük Çamlıca

This park is set at Istanbul's highest point, with spectacular city views. *Map V5 • Dolmuş (minibus) or taxi from Üsküdar*

### 7 Church of the Holy Cross (Surp Haç Kilisesi)

One of several Armenian churches in Üsküdar, the Church of the Holy Cross was built in 1697. Istanbul has an Armenian population of around 60,000 – less than a quarter of what it was during the Ottoman era. *Selamsız Kozanoğlu Sok 3, Üsküdar • (0216) 333 02 50*

### 8 Moda

One of the most fashionable areas of Asian Istanbul, Moda is a favourite haunt of locals on Sunday afternoons, when crowds flock to its cafés, restaurants, boutiques and ice cream shops. *Map C6 • Ferry to Kadıköy, then tram*

### 9 Bağdat Caddesi

A window-shopper's dream, it boasts a host of top fashion stores, including Louis Vuitton, French Connection and Tommy Hilfiger – as well as Turkish chains such as Koton. *Map U6 • Ferry to Kadıköy then taxi or dolmuş*

### 10 Kuzguncuk

Wander through the streets of wooden houses in Istanbul's old Jewish quarter and stop in to see the painted ceiling at Beth Yaakov Synagogue – one of several synagogues on the main street, İcadiye Caddesi. *Map C5*

Interior of Çiya

| **Price Categories** | |
|---|---|
| For a typical meal of *meze* and main course for one without alcohol, and including taxes and extra charges. | **$** under $7<br>**$$** $7–13<br>**$$$** $13–18<br>**$$$$** $18–28<br>**$$$$$** over $28 |

# Top 10 Bars, Cafés and Restaurants

### 1 Kanaat, Üskudar

This traditional *lokanta* is as popular today as when it opened in 1933. It offers inexpensive but excellent Turkish food and very tempting puddings. *Selmanipak Cad 9 • Map X2 • (0216) 553 37 91 • $$*

### 2 Çiya, Kadıköy

The kebabs in this informal restaurant are wonderful – the salads and *meze* are worth a look, too. There are tables on the street and the roof terrace. *Caferağa Mah, Guneşlibahçe Sok 32 • Map U5 • (0216) 418 51 15 • $*

### 3 Otantik, Kadıköy

Otantik offers no-frills, hearty Anatolian cuisine with *gözleme* (stuffed crêpes), fresh chicken, lamb casseroles and stuffed cabbage leaves. *Muvakkithane Cad 62–4 • Map U5 • (0216) 330 71 44 • $$*

### 4 Kadife Sokak, Kadıköy

Known to locals simply as Barlar Sokak ("Bar Street"), this is bursting with bars, cafés, restaurants and clubs catering mainly to the young. Listen to avant-garde jazz or electronica in Karga, taste fine wines in the garden at Isis, or simply sit back and chill in Arka Oda. *Map U5*

### 5 Buddha Rock Bar, Kadıköy

This is a popular student bar, offering a range of cheap drinks, an energetic crowd, and live rock and blues alternating with a DJ. *Caferağa Mah, Kadife Sok 14 • Map U5 • (0216) 345 87 98 • $$*

### 6 Sayla Mantı, Kadıköy

This low-key restaurant serves excellent Turkish ravioli. *Bahariye Cad, Nailbey Sok 32 • Map U5 • (0216) 449 08 42 • $*

### 7 Deniz Yıldızi, Kadıköy

Allow yourself time to sit and watch the boats from this old restaurant-bar on the sea-front. Open all day, the Denizati serves sandwiches and salads, beer and coffee – plus a full restaurant menu. *İskele Cad, Eski Kadıköy İskelesi • Map U5 • (0216) 414 76 43 • $$$*

### 8 Tarihi Moda İskelesi, Moda

In an ornate little building on the old quayside, this café serves decent food and is a perfect spot for breakfast. *At the far end of the pier, off Moda İskele Cad • Map U6 • $$$*

### 9 Hatay Meyhane, Bostancı

A hugely atmospheric tavern, its walls covered in fading photos, the Hatay serves a menu with no fewer than 40 kinds of *meze* from the Antakya region near Turkey's border with Syria. You'll need to book a table at weekends. *Bağdat Cad 526 • (0216) 361 33 57 • $$$*

### 10 Zanzibar, Caddebostan

From Waldorf salad to pizza, the offerings at this trendy restaurant set in a 19th-century seafront mansion are decidedly Westernized. The desserts are scrumptious, as are the views. *Cemil Topuzlu Cad 102/A • (0216) 385 64 30 • $$$*

# STREETSMART

Left **Customs sign** Centre **Tourists waiting outside a mosque** Right **September in Istanbul**

# TOP 10 Planning Your Visit

### 1 Tourist Offices Abroad

Turkey has tourist offices in many cities around the globe, including London, Paris, Rome, Madrid, Los Angeles and New York.

### 2 Turkish Embassies and Consulates

Several countries have Turkish embassies and consulates. The embassy staff will direct you to the consulate if it isn't in the same building.

### 3 Visas and Passports

To enter Turkey you need a full passport valid for at least six months. Citizens of the following countries require visas, paid for in hard currency at the point of entry into Turkey: UK (£10), Canada (US$60), Australia (US$20), USA (US$20) and Ireland (€10). Photos are not required. You receive a multiple-entry tourist visa valid for three months. South Africans or people with British National Overseas passports must apply for a visa at a consulate before travelling. New Zealand nationals receive a free tourist visa on arrival, valid for up to three months.

### 4 Duty-Free Allowances

Visitors may bring 50 cigars, 200 cigarettes, 200 g pipe tobacco, 5 litres wine or spirits, 5 x 100 ml bottles of perfume, 1 kg sweets and 1 kg chocolate, 500 g tea, 1.5 kg coffee and 1.5 kg instant coffee into Turkey. You may also buy 400 cigarettes, 100 cigars and 500 g pipe tobacco from the Turkish duty-free shops on arrival. Penalties for possessing narcotics are very harsh.

### 5 Travel Insurance

You are strongly advised to take out travel insurance with full medical cover, including repatriation by air. If buying a Europe-only policy, check that it will also cover you on the Asian side of Istanbul.

### 6 Inoculations

Before travelling to Istanbul make sure your basic inoculations are up-to-date, and check with your doctor about hepatitis A and hepatitis B vaccinations.

### 7 Climate

Summers are sunny and dry, with the odd thunderstorm. It can reach 40° C (104° F), but 31–3° C (88–91° F) is normal at noon in August, dropping to around 23° C (74° F) at night. Winter can be cool and damp, with a little snow and likely January temperatures of around 8° C (46° F) at midday and 2° C (36° F) overnight.

### 8 When to Go

In May, June and September the weather is pleasant and there are fewer tourists than usual. In November or February, prices are slashed.

### 9 What to Pack

In summer, pack light clothes for the midday heat with a jacket for the evenings, plus a hat and sunblock. In winter, take a coat and umbrella. To visit mosques, wear long trousers or a skirt that covers the knees, and a shirt that covers the shoulders. Women should also bring a scarf with which to cover the head. Don't forget to bring mosquito repellent and an adaptor plug.

### 10 Choosing an Area

Sultanahmet has charming hotels, great restaurants and easy access to key sights. If you are a night owl, stay in Beyoğlu, where you'll find most of the best restaurants and clubs. For peace and quiet, stay in the Bosphorus villages.

### Turkish Embassies Abroad

**Australia**
*(06) 295 02 27/8*

**Canada**
*(613) 789 4044/3440*

**Ireland**
*(0353) 1668 5240*

**New Zealand**
*(04) 472 1290/2*

**South Africa**
*(012) 342 60 53/4/5*

**UK**
*(020) 7393 0202*

**USA**
*(212) 949 0159*


Preceding pages **Carpet-seller in the Grand Bazaar**

Left **Train at Sirkeci Station** Centre **Inter-city coach from Esenler** Right **Ferries at Karaköy**

# Top 10 Getting to Istanbul

### 1 International Flights

The national carrier, Turkish Airlines, flies to and from more than 100 airports worldwide. Other major airlines and low-cost carriers also fly to Istanbul. Flights are 3.5 hours from London and 9 hours from New York. *Turkish Airlines: (0212) 444 08 49 (central reservations) • www.thy.com*

### 2 Domestic Flights

Turkish Airlines competes with domestic operators including Onur Air, Atlas Jet and Fly Air.

### 3 Airports

Istanbul has two main airports, Atatürk International and Sabiha Gökçen. Most major airlines fly into Atatürk International, 24 km (15 miles) west of the city centre, on the European shore. Sabiha Gökçen, on the Asian side, is 50 km (30 miles) from Taksim. A few larger carriers such as Japan Air Lines (JAL) and Air France fly here, as does the UK budget airline easyJet.

### 4 Airport–City Links

Atatürk International has good transport links. Taxis and hotel buses are fixed-price (taxis around US$15–20). Havaş buses run at 30-minute intervals to Akmerkez (Etiler, 45 minutes) and Taksim (about 40 minutes). An airport bus also meets the boat at Bakırköy and the metro connects the airport with Sultanahmet and (via the funicular) with Taksim. From Sabiha Gökçen buses link with ferries to/from Bostancı, 14 km (9 miles) from the airport. A costly taxi ride is the only other option, which could wipe out the benefit of a budget flight.

### 5 Trains

You can travel to Istanbul by train – from Western Europe or from Moscow – but it is a two- or three-day trip. Inter-rail, Eurodomino and Balkan Flexipass tickets are valid in Turkey, but Eurail passes are not. *Rail Europe: 0870 837 13 71 (in UK); 1-877 257 28 87 (in US) • www.rail europe.co.uk (UK); www. raileurope.com (US)*

### 6 Train Stations

International trains and those from European Turkey use Sirkeci Station, Eminönü; trains from Anatolia come into Haydarpaşa Station on the Asian shore. *Train information: (0212) 527 00 50 (European lines); (0216) 336 20 63 (Asian lines) • www.tcdd.gov.tr*

### 7 Coaches

Coaches travel to Istanbul from all over Europe. In the UK, contact Eurolines. Coaches within Turkey are comfortable and popular but ticket prices are complicated. *Eurolines: (0870) 580 80 80 • www.eurolines.co.uk*

### 8 Coach Stations

Istanbul's main coach station is at Esenler, about 10 km (6 miles) northwest of the city centre. There is a second station at Harem, just behind Haydarpaşa Station on the Asian shore. *(0212) 658 05 05 (Esenler); (0216) 553 37 63 (Harem)*

### 9 Ferries

Ferries run to Turkey from Italy, Greece and Northern Cyprus. The UKR Ferry Shipping Company runs a regular ferry across the Black Sea from Odessa. *www.ukrferry. com (UKR); www.ido.com.tr (Istanbul Fast Ferries)*

### 10 Cruises

Istanbul is not on the Mediterranean schedule of all the major cruise companies, but most of them come into the city a few times a year, including P&O, Swan Hellenic, Costa Cruises and MSC Cruises. *www.pocruises.com; www.swanhellenic.com; www.costacruises.com; www.msccruises.com*

#### Istanbul Airports

**Atatürk International**
*Havalimani Baş Müdürlüğü • (0212) 463 30 00 • www.ataturk airport.com*

**Istanbul Sabiha Gökçen International**
*Pendik (Asian Side) • (0216) 585 50 00 • www.sgairport.com*

Left **Licensed yellow *taksi*** Centre **Ferry** Right **Modern tram, Sultanahmet**

# TOP 10 Getting Around Istanbul

**1 Taxis**
A licensed taxi *(taksi)* is yellow and shows a light on top when available for hire. Before you set off, always check that the meter is switched on. Better still, fix the fare before you get in. Ask a local what the fare should be and haggle hard *(see p111)*. There should be no change in taxi prices from day to night. If you cross the Bosphorus, the bridge toll will be added to your fare.

**2 Dolmuş**
These cheap, shared minibus taxis run along set routes, and will only depart when they are full (really full – dolmuş means "stuffed") but will pick up or set down where you want along the route. Ranks have a blue sign with a black D on a white background. They don't operate in the city centre.

**3 Metro**
There are two metro sections: one runs from Levent to Taksim, the other from Aksaray via Kocatepe to the airport. The metro is being extended under the Golden Horn to connect with Yenikapı.

**4 Tram**
The tram is a small but splendid affair that runs from the airport through the old city, across the Galata Bridge and along the Bosphorus to Dolmabahçe Palace, linking to Taksim via the funicular. It is cheap, frequent, air-conditioned and it beats the traffic. It operates 6am–midnight daily. The Nostalgic Tram *(see p82)* runs along İstiklal Caddesi between Taksim and Tünel, and along Bahariye cad between Kadıköy and Moda.

**5 Funiculars**
The Tünel, connecting Galata to Beyoğlu, is one of the world's oldest undergrounds *(see p82)*. A second funicular runs from the Bosphorus shore (at Kabataş) to Taksim.

**6 Tickets**
Buy tokens from kiosks near stations and stops. If you are around for more than a couple of days, get an Istanbul Card that can be used on all buses (except double-deckers), trams, the metro and ferries. Just lower your card to the reader as you enter whichever form of public transport you are taking, and recharge it when necessary. The deposit for the card is 6 TL and you can load money from kiosks, stations or vending machines.
• *Transport information: www.iett.gov.tr*

**7 Ferries**
The main ferry docks are at Eminönü. There are others at Karaköy and Kabataş. A useful route runs along the Marmara coast to Bakırköy, from where there is a shuttle bus to the airport *(see p103)*. There are regular sailings from Eminönü to Kadıköy and Üsküdar on the Asian side, but the most scenic way to cross is on the Bosphorus ferry *(see pp28–9)*. Called *vapur*, these boats are run by the Istanbul Seabus Company (İDO).
• *(0212) 444 44 36*
• *www.ido.com.tr*

**8 By Car**
Driving in the city centre is a nightmare. If you have come to Istanbul by car, use the ring roads that skirt the city centre and park as soon as possible. The larger business hotels have parking, but those in the old city do not. To take in sights spread out around the city walls, Golden Horn or along the Bosphorus, hire a car and driver – most hotels can arrange this for you.

**9 On Foot**
You will miss many of the best aspects of the city, such as the small alleys and markets, if you don't walk. Wear shoes that you can slip on and off easily for mosques. Traffic will only stop at light-controlled crossings.

**10 Tours**
There are plenty of tours on offer, by bus, car or on foot *(see p105)*. Look out, too, for short breaks to sights such as Gallipoli and Troy, Edirne or Bursa *(see pp52–3)*.



*There are few radio-controlled taxi networks, but staff in hotels, restaurants and shops are always happy to find a cab for you.*

Left **Galeri Kayseri bookshop** Centre ***The Guide*** Right **Tourist office, Sultanahmet**

# Top 10 Sources of Information

### 1 Tourist Offices in Istanbul

There are several official tourist offices and kiosks around the city. Most staff speak English.

### 2 Websites

For travel advice, visit www.mfa.gov.tr (Turkish Foreign Ministry); for the latest travel health advice, go to www.mdtravelhealth.com. For tourist information, see www.tourismturkey.org (the Ministry of Tourism), www.gototurkey.co.uk (the Turkish Tourist Office in London), www.istanbul.com (the official Istanbul Tourist Office), www.kultur.gov.tr (the Turkish Ministry of Culture and Tourism) and www.nisanyan.net (a listing of small hotels). The definitive US-run Turkey tour site is www.turkeytravelplanner.com.

### 3 Magazines

*The Guide* (bi-monthly) and *Time Out* (monthly) have entertainment and dining listings. *Istanbul Forever* is a bi-monthly magazine available free in hotels. *Cornucopia* covers the arts, history and general culture of Turkey. *www.theguideturkey.com; www.cornucopia.net*

### 4 Newspapers

The bestsellers are *Sabah* and *Hürriyet*. The English-language paper, *Turkish Daily News*, prints entertainment listings. You can get day-old international papers at major hotels and kiosks in tourist areas. *www.turkishdailynews.com*

### 5 Foreign-Language Bookshops

There are several shops offering books in English and other languages, but centrally located Galeri Kayseri is the main English-language retailer. For second-hand books, look in the Book Bazaar in Beyazıt *(see p70)*. *www.galerikayseri.com*

### 6 Maps

The free city map available from tourist offices and most hotels is all that most people need. For more detail, look for the Freytag & Berndt Istanbul City Map (scale 1:10,000).

### 7 Private Guides

Most travel agents and tour operators in Turkey will be happy to provide a private guide in one of half a dozen major languages. The guide should be accredited by the Ministry of Tourism.

### 8 Guided Tours

There are tours by bus, boat, on foot or a mix of them, with full- and half-day options. Plan Tours do an open-topped double-decker bus tour of the city that can be a good way to get your bearings. There are also tours by night and trips to cultural evenings – including belly dancing.

### 9 Government Advice

The UK Foreign Office and US State Department websites give detailed, up-to-date advice on the risks of travel. *www.fco.gov.uk (UK); www.travel.state.gov (US)*

### 10 Finding Your Way Around

Getting around is not always easy – make sure you have full directions and a map before you set off. Write your destination down and show it to the driver or a passerby – chances are they won't understand your accent. Give/get directions by district first, nearest major landmark next, then the street. Once you are in the vicinity, ask and keep on asking.

### Tourist Offices

**Sultanahmet**
*At Meydanı • (0212) 518 18 02/87 54*

**Beyazıt**
*Beyazıt Meydanı • (0212) 522 49 02*

### Guided Tour Operators

**Plan Tours, Elmadağ**
*Cumhuriyet Caddesi 131/1 • (0212) 234 77 77 • www.plantours.com*

**Viking Turizm, Taksim**
*Mete Caddesi 18 • (0212) 334 26 00 • www.vikingturizm.com.tr*

*Other travel health websites include www.thehtd.org/content/travel.asp and www.masta-travel-health.com*

Left **Public phone kiosks** Centre **PTT logo** Right **Blue Mosque lit for Ramazan celebrations**

# TOP 10 Practicalities

### 1 Time
Turkey is 3 hours ahead of Greenwich Mean Time in summer (March–October) and 2 hours ahead for the rest of the year.

### 2 Electricity
The current is 220V, and plugs have two round pins. You'll need a transformer to use 110V appliances from the US.

### 3 Opening Hours
Banks open 8:30am–noon and 1:30–5pm Monday to Friday; a few larger branches also open on Saturday mornings. All have 24-hour cash dispensers. Post offices open 9am–5pm Monday to Saturday. Shops are open 10am–6pm Monday to Saturday, with some local stores, malls and large shops open longer. Museums are usually open 9am–5pm (closed Monday or Tuesday).

### 4 Public Holidays
In addition to the five state holidays, there are two principal religious festivals: Şeker Bayramı, which follows the holy month of Ramazan (Ramadan in other countries), and Kurban Bayramı *(see pp46–7)*. During Ramazan, no water or food is allowed to touch the lips during daylight hours. Nothing actually shuts down, but daily life is disrupted (although the parties at night can be spectacular). The dates of Ramazan, Şeker Bayramı and Kurban Bayramı move backwards by 11 days each year. Christmas Day is not a Muslim festival, but is still celebrated by a large number of Turks.

### 5 Post and Couriers
Post offices and boxes can be recognized by a yellow and blue PTT logo. Stamps can only be bought at post offices and PTT kiosks. The post can be slow, so if you want to send purchases home, use a courier firm for speed – all the main courier companies have offices in Istanbul.

### 6 Internet
Most tourist hotels, of any standard, have a computer with free Internet access in the lobby. Many also offer free Wi-Fi, as do some cafés.

### 7 Telephone
Turkey's mobile phone system is compatible with UK phones, but US cellphones may not work. To save on charges, buy a local pay-as-you-go SIM card or an international card such as sim4travel. Public phones accept credit cards or a phone card bought from a post office. Hotel phones are usually expensive.
*www.sim4travel.co.uk*

### 8 Dialling Codes
The international dialling code for Turkey is 90. Istanbul has two area codes: 0212 for the European side, 0216 for the Asian side.

### 9 Language
In tourist areas there will always be someone who speaks some English. Written Turkish uses the Western alphabet, but there are some differences in pronunciation. C is pronounced "*j*" as in "jam"; ç is "*ch*" as in "church". S is as in snake; ş is "*sh*" as in "shut". İ is used as in igloo; the dotless "i" (ı) is more like "*uh*". The ğ is silent, but is used to draw out the preceding vowel. So *Cağaloğlu* is actually pronounced *jar-low-loo*.

### 10 Photography
You are allowed to take photos inside most major monuments and museums, but flash is usually banned and in a few places they also bar tripods. There may be a photographic charge on top of the entry fee.

#### State Holidays

**1 January**
*New Year's Day*

**23 April**
*National Sovereignty & Children's Day*

**19 May**
*Youth & Sports Day*

**30 August**
*Victory Day*

**29 October**
*Republic Day*

*Power sockets are often in short supply in hotel rooms, so if you have a laptop, phone and camera to charge, bring a multi-plug.*

Left **50-Turkish-lira note** Centre **ATM** Right **Tipping is customary in restaurants**

# TOP 10 Money

### 1 Currency

The Turkish lira comes in 5, 10, 20, 50, 100 and 200 TL notes and 1 TL coins. One TL is split into 100 kuruş, which come in 5, 10, 25 and 50 kuruş coins. New notes and coins were issued in 2009 when the New Turkish Lira (YTL) became obsolete. You are allowed to bring unlimited foreign currency and up to US$5,000-worth of TL into Turkey, but you'll probably get a better exchange rate if you wait until you are in Turkey to exchange your money.

### 2 Small Change

Make sure that you have plenty of small-denomination notes and coins with you at all times, as few traders seem to have any and many will assume that you don't actually want any change from a larger note. Cab drivers may compound this by sleight of hand *(see p111)*.

### 3 Using Foreign Currency

Most souvenir shops are happy to accept lira, US dollars, euros or pounds sterling. Your change will come in lira.

### 4 ATMs and Banks

There are plenty of banks, but changing money can be slow. The many 24-hour cash dispensers (ATMs) accept all Maestro and Cirrus bank cards with a PIN number, and will also give a cash advance on credit cards. Most are programmed with several languages, but pay out only in Turkish lira.

### 5 Exchange Offices

If you have cash to exchange, the best place to go is an exchange office *(döviz)*. These kiosks are found in all the main tourist areas. They are faster and usually offer a better rate of exchange than the banks. They rarely accept traveller's cheques.

### 6 Credit Cards

Most outlets dealing with tourists will accept major credit cards such as Visa and MasterCard. American Express cards are less popular because commission is higher. You may be asked to pay a premium to cover the cost of the commission.

### 7 Traveller's Cheques

You can cash traveller's cheques at foreign exchange desks at banks and post offices and at American Express and Thomas Cook offices, but few outlets, including hotels, will accept them.

### 8 Haggling

Turkey is extremely good value for visitors. The only exception is fuel, which is very expensive. However, haggling for a bargain is part of daily life, and in places like the Grand Bazaar and the old city it's a necessity. Take your time, shop around and don't feel pressurized. When you are ready, offer half the price and take it from there. Don't be afraid to haggle for a fixed-price taxi ride, either, but don't expect to bargain for goods in upmarket shops.

### 9 VAT and VAT Refunds

VAT (KDV in Turkish) is included in fixed-price goods. There are various rates, but the most common is 18 per cent. Prices may rise if you ask for a VAT invoice – a trader who writes an invoice will have to pay tax. To reclaim tax on departure, shop at places displaying a tax-free sign and get a Global Refund Cheque to reclaim the tax (in cash) at the airport. You may be asked to produce the goods, so keep them with you.

### 10 Tipping

A service charge may be included *(servis dahil)* at a restaurant. If it is not, leave 10 per cent. There are no set rates for hotel staff, but at least 5 TL for porters and room cleaners (daily) is acceptable. Hamam attendants will generally expect up to 10 per cent of the price. Don't tip taxi drivers.

*Where possible, get your hotel rate quoted in Turkish lira not dollars – you'll save money.*

Left **Bottled water** Centre **Pharmacy sign** Right **Police car**

# Top 10 Security and Health

### 1 Water and Food Hygiene

While Istanbul tap water is considered safe, it is advisable to drink bottled water. The standard of hygiene in most cafés and restaurants is good.

### 2 Avoiding Bugs

If you are vulnerable to stomach upsets, foods to avoid include salad, seafood from street stalls and unpackaged ice cream. If you do get a bug, don't eat for 24 hours, then try 24 hours on black tea, water, yoghurt and dry bread. If you still feel ill, seek medical assistance.

### 3 Medical Assistance

A pharmacy *(eczane)* can treat minor ailments and many drugs are available over the counter, without prescription. In every district one pharmacist will be open around the clock for emergencies, with the rota *(nöbetçi)* posted in all pharmacists' windows. All hotels will call a doctor for you. There are also good free public clinics (*poliklinik*) for minor problems.

### 4 Hospitals

Istanbul has public and private hospitals – the latter tend to offer a higher standard of medical care and cleanliness.

### 5 ID

It is illegal to be out in public without photo ID. If all you have is your passport and you don't wish to risk carrying it around, take a photocopy of the relevant page.

### 6 Crime

Istanbul has very low crime levels compared to most major cities. Take normal precautions. If you feel threatened, raise your voice and ask locals for help *(see also p111)*.

### 7 Terrorist Threat

Turkey has suffered bombing campaigns by PKK Kurdish nationalists and al-Qaeda. PKK bombs have targeted suburban districts and coastal resorts. Al-Qaeda bombs have been more central, hitting synagogues, the British Consulate and the HSBC bank in Istanbul.

### 8 Emergency Phone Numbers

Emergency service operators may not speak English. Ask a Turk to call for you or contact the Tourist Police.

### 9 Police

The Turkish police are trying hard to improve their image and, as long as you don't break the law, they will be polite and helpful. In tourist areas, report losses, theft or other problems at the Tourist Police office. *Tourism Police, Yerebatan Caddesi 6, Sultanahmet • (0212) 527 45 03 • Open 24hrs daily (translators present 8:30am–5pm Mon–Fri) • www.iem.gov.tr*

### 10 Consulates

While embassies are situated in the Turkish capital of Ankara, most countries still maintain consulates in Istanbul. These should be your first stop in case of trouble – they will assist with missing documents, arrange repatriation, or help you to find legal representation if needed.

### Emergency Numbers

**Police**
*155*

**Ambulance**
*112*

**Fire**
*110*

**General Emergency**
*115*

*Hospitals*

**Amerikan Hastanesi**
*Güzelbahçe Sokak 20, Nişantaşı Map C4 • (0212) 444 37 77*

**Florence Nightingale Hastanesi**
*Abide-i Hürriyet Caddesi 164, Çağlayan, Şişli • Map T4 • (0212) 224 49 50*

**International Hospital**
*İstanbul Caddesi 82, Yeşilköy • (0212) 663 3000 or (0212) 468 44 44*

**Acıbadem Hastanesi**
*Tekin Sokak 8, Kadıköy, (Asian side) • (0216) 544 44 44*

*Turkey has no medical agreements with other countries. You'll have to pay for treatment and claim it back on your insurance.*

Left **Turkish women wearing head scarves** Right **"No Smoking" sign**



# Top 10 Special Concerns

### 1 Children
Children are welcome almost everywhere, but give very blond children a hat or they will attract uncomfortable levels of attention. Some large hotels arrange activities for children, and most will provide babysitting on request.

### 2 Babies
Be sure to pack plenty of supplies. You can get everything you need in Istanbul, from nappies to baby food, but it isn't always easy to find them in tourist areas since supermarkets tend to be in the suburbs.

### 3 Women
Some Turkish women wear strappy tops and short skirts, but a growing number are returning to wearing scarves. A few – often Arab tourists – wear full burkas. Western women are seen as free and easy – Turkish men will flirt and younger women will be hassled, but you can usually stop it with a polite but firm response. Wear clothes that cover the shoulders and knees, walk purposefully and avoid quiet streets at night if alone.

### 4 Gay Travellers
Homosexuality is not illegal in Turkey, but it is frowned upon by Islam. There is a thriving gay scene in Istanbul, but locals are not always far out of the closet and there is significant homophobia. Don't be too demonstrative in public and be careful where you go on nights out; some local gay bars are decidedly seedy. But there are many safe venues in Beyoğlu and several useful websites including www.trgi.info.

### 5 Disabled Travellers
On the whole, the city is difficult to navigate in a wheelchair. Older, historic buildings tend to be totally or partially inaccessible and many mosques refuse access to wheelchairs. But the biggest problem is Istanbul itself – with its seven, often steep, hills and cobbled roads and pavements. The Turkish Tourist Office in London publishes a helpful guide to facilities for disabled travellers.

### 6 Older Travellers
You are guaranteed courteous service and assistance – Turkish people revere seniors. At monuments and museums, look out for over-65 discounts.

### 7 Student and Youth Travellers
There are three hostels accredited by Hostelling International. A 50 per cent reduction on entry to museums and monuments is possible with an ISIC (International Student Identity Card). This will also give you intercity train discounts. Discounts may also be possible with a WYSE (World Youth Student and Educational) Travel Confederation card (formerly the FIYTO).
*www.hihostels.com* • *www.aboutwysetc.org* • *www.isic.org*

### 8 Religion
Ninety-nine per cent of Turks are Muslim, but the degree to which they practise their religion varies greatly. There are some fundamentalists, but the vast majority believe utterly in a secular state and are completely tolerant of other religions.

### 9 Smoking
The Turks smoke a lot of pungent black Turkish tobacco. However, smoking is prohibited in most enclosed public areas, including taxis, ferries, trains and also shopping centres. The ban also applies to cafés, bars and restaurants.

### 10 Export Regulations
Any object over 100 years old needs a certificate of permission to be exported. Museums usually issue these on behalf of the Ministry of Culture; a reputable dealer should arrange the paperwork for you. If you attempt to smuggle out antiquities you will find yourself facing large fine or even a jail sentence.

*Istanbul has plenty of safe, open spaces where you can take your children to run around and let off steam.*

Left **Saray *muhallebici*** Centre **Typical *lokanta* fare** Right **A nargile café**

# Top 10 Eating and Accommodation Tips

### 1 Types of Restaurant

*Lokantas* are day-to-day eateries. They range from self-service cafeterias to full-service brasserie-style places. Prices are affordable, but few serve alcohol. A cheap self-service café may also be known as a *bufé*. The *restoran* is upmarket; if the word *balık* is included, the place specializes in fish and seafood.

### 2 Fast Food

The *kebapcı* serves kebabs and *lahmacun*, a sort of thin pancake with a savoury topping; the *dönerci*, döner kebabs and other roast meat. The *pideci* is the Turkish equivalent of a pizzeria.

### 3 Meyhanes, Nargile and Other Cafés

If you fancy a drink and live music with a meal, try a *meyhane*. If you want to chill out in a haze of smoke, head for a *nargile* café, where you'll be plied with sweet tea while you suck on a hubble-bubble waterpipe. The simple *kahvehane* (tea room) is generally a male preserve, where men, spend their time playing games of backgammon. Some cafés have a separate section for women and families *(aile salonu)* at the back, as do some restaurants. Local bars in central Istanbul are often rather grim. If you want to go for a drink, the best choice is a tourist hotel.

### 4 Vegetarian Food

Few restaurants in Istanbul cater specifically to vegetarians, but while vegetarian *(veciteryan)* main courses are rare, staff are generally helpful and most places serve a selection of vegetable *meze* which can make a delicious main meal.

### 5 Muhallebicis and Pastanes

A *muhallebici* sells milk puddings; *pastanes* sell pastries, such as *baklava*, to take away.

### 6 Choosing Your Meal

In central Istanbul, many restaurants have menus in several languages, but off the beaten track ordering a meal is more difficult. Try the "show and point" method – the waiter brings a tray of *meze* and you indicate the ones you want. For the main course try using a phrase book *(see pp126–7)*, or ask your hotel concierge to write down some recommended dishes for you.

### 7 Choosing a Hotel

On the whole, the standard of hotels is high. The government-run star system is based on facilities, not on a hotel's atmosphere or efficiency – so don't rely on stars alone. There are online booking services, many with discounts. The US site www.tripadvisor.com offers honest reviews by other travellers.

### 8 Guesthouses and B&Bs

The dividing line between guesthouse, pension and small hotel is blurred in Turkey. There are family-run guesthouses but – with literally one or two exceptions owned and run by foreigners – there is no equivalent of the British bed & breakfast (B&B), or the French *chambre d'hôte*, where you lodge and dine with a local family. Self-catering apartments are only just starting to take off.

### 9 Out of Season

Istanbul stays open year round, but prices drop dramatically out of season (Nov–Mar, excluding Christmas). Hotels are available for between one-third and one-half of their rack rate. Even shopping prices come down.

### 10 Special Hotels

The charming places categorized as "special hotels" are usually in Istanbul's many restored buildings. They are generally small and often the nicest places to stay. However, rooms may also be small, there might not be a lift, and there may be a shower rather than a bathtub. Service is usually excellent and the desk staff, at least, normally speak good English. Special hotels are also being joined now by a sprinkling of stylish boutique hotels.

*Vegetarians should note that even "vegetarian" dishes may contain some meat – ask if they are "etsiz" (meat-free).*

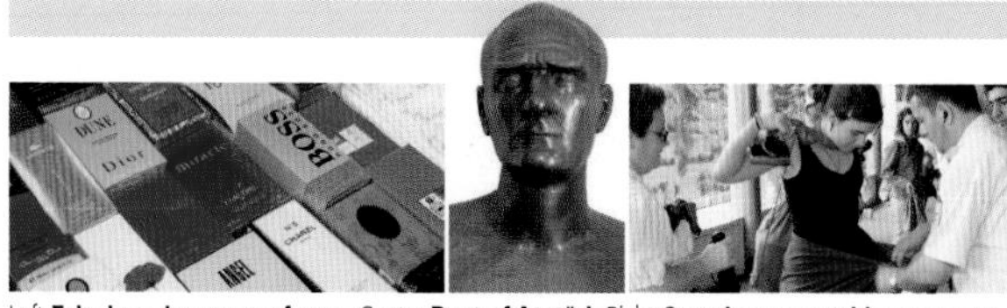


Left **Fake brand-name perfumes** Centre **Bust of Atatürk** Right **Covering up outside a mosque**

# TOP 10 Things to Avoid

### 1 Drugs

Turkey is used as a staging post by traffickers from Afghanistan and Iran, and street drugs, though not a major part of the local culture, are available to those who want them. Penalties for trafficking or possession are extremely harsh. Never agree to carry things home for other people – Turks or fellow travellers.

### 2 Fakes

There is a thriving industry creating fakes, from carpets and Roman coins to Rolex watches and Gucci bags. If you are happy to have a fake and it is sold as such, that's fine. But if you are spending serious money, be sure to do so at a reputable outlet and that your purchase comes with full provenance.

### 3 Unscrupulous Cab Drivers

Most cab drivers are fine, but some, particularly in the old city, charge three times the going rate and try to cheat on payment, pretending, for instance, that the 50 TL note you just gave them was only 5 TL. Inspect every note and say what it is out loud as you hand it over – also keep small notes at all times, as the drivers will rarely have change.

### 4 Prostitutes

Most nightclubs in Turkey are sleazy places. There is a thriving trade in women from former Soviet states (called "natashas" by locals). Chances are that the woman sidling up to you will prove a ruinous proposition, not only in inflated drink prices (over $1,000 for the evening, quoted by some) but also in hospital visits later on.

### 5 Marriage Proposals

Turkish men have a taste for soulful romance delivered with a twinkle in the eye. Enjoy, but keep it light. All too many women fall for the banter only to discover a couple of years down the line that the real draw was their EU or US passport. If you think you have found true romance, take it slowly and make sure.

### 6 Earthquakes

Istanbul is on an earthquake belt and it rumbles regularly: the last major quake was in 1999 when, tragically, more than 23,000 people died in Greater Istanbul. But large quakes are few and far between. If one does occur while you are there, keep calm, make sure you have shelter and drinkable water, and try to make contact with your consulate.

### 7 Pickpockets

Pickpockets and muggers operate in the market streets around the Grand Bazaar. Take the precautions normal for a crowded city – carry a handbag with a zip and a cross-shoulder strap, put your wallet in the front pocket of your jeans, and stay aware.

### 8 Criticizing Turkey

The Turks have great national pride and no sense of humour when it comes to their country. Criticizing Turkey in any way is a huge social faux pas. It is actually illegal to show disrespect to Atatürk, the Turkish government, flag or the security services.

### 9 Offending Islamic Sensibilities

As Islamic societies go, Turkey is very laid back but, while it is not necessary to dress from head to toe in basic black, you should respect the culture and beliefs *(see p39)*. Avoid public displays of affection between couples and, above all, do not make jokes about Islam.

### 10 Traditional-Style Public Conveniences

The number and cleanliness of modern public conveniences (*bay* for men, *bayan* for women) has improved hugely in recent years, but there are still some traditional "squat" toilets around. However, most sights, cafés and restaurants have excellent facilities. Tip an attendant 50 kuruş. Carry tissues as there may not always be paper.

*Don't accept free drinks from strangers – people have been offered spiked beer or cola, then robbed.*

Left **Çırağan Palace Kempinski** Centre **Four Seasons** Right **Conrad Istanbul**

# Top 10 Luxury Hotels

### 1 Çırağan Palace Kempinski, Beşiktaş

Its terrace lapped by the Bosphorus, this Ottoman palace has a spa, health club and two of the city's best restaurants. Most of the 313 rooms are in the modern extensions, but for a real treat take one of the 11 suites in the original palace. *Çırağan Cad 32 • Map C4 • (0212) 326 46 46 • www.kempinski.com/istanbul • $$$$$*

### 2 Four Seasons Hotel, Sultanahmet

The sheer opulence of the Four Seasons belies its past as an Ottoman prison. The 65 rooms are exquisitely furnished with antiques and *kilims*, there is a health club for the virtuous and sybaritic alike, a magnificent glass-roofed restaurant and superb views over the Sea of Marmara. *Tevkifhane Sok 1 • Map R5 • (0212) 638 82 00 • www.fourseasons.com • $$$$$*

### 3 Eresin Crown, Sultanahmet

Standing on the site of the great Byzantine Palace, this truly luxurious hotel even has its own museum. All 60 rooms and suites have parquet floors and Jacuzzi baths. There are two restaurants, a bar and a terrace with fine sea views. *Küçük Ayasofya Cad 40 • Map R4 • (0212) 638 44 28 • www.eresincrown.com.tr • $$$$$*

### 4 Ceylan Intercontinental, Taksim

This hilltop tower offers some of the finest views in a city where peerless views are commonplace. It has 382 rooms and suites, bar, restaurants, terrace, health club and 24-hour business centre. Join Istanbul high society for tea with live music in the botanic garden or tea lounge. *Asker Ocağı Cad 1 • Map B5 • (0212) 368 44 44 • www.interconti.com.tr • $$$$$*

### 5 Hyatt Regency, Taksim

A resort hotel with 360 rooms and suites, the Hyatt has a health club, pool, tennis courts and business facilities, as well as elegant decor and great views. *Taşkışla Cad • Map B5 • (0212) 368 12 34 • www.istanbul.hyatt.com • $$$$$*

### 6 Conrad Istanbul, Beşiktaş

Each of the 590 rooms in this huge, S-shaped hotel has a view. The facilities are second-to-none, and the furnishings chic. Its bars and restaurants offer Italian and Turkish cuisine. *Yıldız Cad, • Map C5 • 0212 227 30 00 • www.conradistanbul.com • $$$$$*

### 7 Marmara Pera Tepebaşı

In the heart of Beyoğlu, with a signature café-restaurant and rooftop pool, this chic hotel has fabulous floor-to-ceiling windows in every room. *Meşrutiyet Caddesi • Map J5 • (0212) 251 46 46 • www.themarmarahotels.com • $$$$$*

### 8 Bosphorus Palace, Beylerbeyi (Asian Side)

This confection of gilt and crystal on the banks of the Bosphorus is the restored *yalı* (mansion) of a 19th-century Grand Vizier. With only 14 rooms, it is intimate as well as glamorous – perfect for a romantic dinner. A private boat commutes to the city centre. *Yalıboyu Cad 64 • Map U4 • (0216) 422 00 03 • www.bosphoruspalace.com • $$$$$*

### 9 Ritz-Carlton, Şişli

"Ritz" is a byword for luxury, and the Istanbul hotel's 244 rooms and suites more than live up to expectation. There are spas for the women, and a whisky and cigar bar for the men. *Süzer Plaza, Elmadağ • Map U4 • (0212) 334 44 44 • www.ritzcarlton.com • $$$$$*

### 10 Central Palace, Taksim

This boutique hotel has 49 spacious rooms, with workstations, Jacuzzis and even steam baths. No alcohol is served or sold, but you can bring your own to your room. *Lamartin Cad 18 • Map B5 • (0212) 313 40 40 • www.thecentralpalace.com • $$$$$*



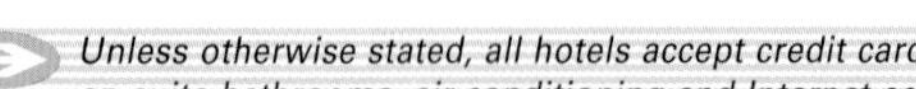
*Unless otherwise stated, all hotels accept credit cards, and have en-suite bathrooms, air conditioning and Internet access.*

**Price Categories**

| For a standard, double room per night (with breakfast if included), taxes and extra charges. | | |
|---|---|---|
| | $ | under $45 |
| | $$ | $45–80 |
| | $$$ | $80–180 |
| | $$$$ | $180–300 |
| | $$$$$ | over $300 |

**Radisson SAS Bosphorus, Ortaköy**

# Top 10 Large Upmarket Hotels

### 1 Germir Palas

It is easy to miss the entrance to this mid-town gem on Üsküdar's main street. The lobby and bars are plush, and the rooms are well decorated with interesting textiles. The terrace restaurant is great in summer, with fine views over the Bosphorous. The street-level Vanilla Café is very stylish. *Cumhuriyet Cad 7, Taksim • Map Y2 •* (0212) 361 11 10 • *www.germirpalas.com • $$$$*

### 2 Taxim Suites, Taksim

These 20 fully serviced suites are good high-end value for those who need a bit more space, giving you a one-bed apartment for less than the cost of a five-star hotel room. With Taksim Square on the doorstep, there are plenty of places to eat nearby. *Cumhuriyet Cad 31 • Map B5 • (0212) 254 77 77 • www.taximsuites.com • $$$$*

### 3 Mövenpick Hotel Istanbul, Levent

This hilltop hotel with 249 rooms and suites offers great views, slick service, good bars and restaurants, and a health club. The top selling-point, however, is the lobby café, with sumptuous chocolates, cakes and Mövenpick ice cream. *Büyükdere Cad 4 Levent • Map U3 • (0212) 319 29 29 • www.movenpickhotels.com • $$$$*

### 4 Radisson SAS Bosphorus Hotel, Ortaköy

The location is the real gem – the peaceful village of Ortaköy, beside the Bosphorus. This hotel has a patio restaurant overlooking the water, and 120 rooms with contemporary decor. Allow plenty of time for taxis into town during rush hour. *Çırağan Cad 46 • Map U4 • (0212) 310 15 00 • www.radissonsas.com • $$$$*

### 5 Polat Renaissance, Yeşilyurt

Near the airport and World Trade Centre, this 416-room hotel has a luxury pool and health club, fine restaurants, bars and cafés, and good business facilities. *Sahilyolu Cad • (0212) 414 18 00 • www.polatrenaissance.com • $$$$$*

### 6 The Marmara Istanbul, Taksim

This large, modern hotel on Taksim Square has 376 comfortable rooms with city views, as well as a fully equipped gym, outdoor pool, *hamam* and several top-class restaurants. *Taksim Meydanı • Map L4 • (0212) 251 46 96 • www.themarmarahotels.com • $$$$$*

### 7 Best Western Eresin Taxim Hotel, Taksim

You can even get hypo-allergenic pillows at this four-star hotel. The 70 rooms and suites include some triples. The lounge bar has live piano music in the evenings. *Topçu Cad 34 • Map B5 • 0212 256 08 03 • www.eresintaxim.com.tr • $$$*

### 8 Swissôtel The Bosphorus, Maçka

Perched on the hilltop, with fabulous Bosphorus views, this is one of the giants, with 585 rooms and suites, wellness centre, shopping arcade, restaurants and rooftop bars. *Bayıldım Cad 34 • Map C5 • (0212) 326 1100 • www.istanbul.swissotel.com • $$$$$*

### 9 Ataköy Marina Hotel

Situated on the shores of the Sea of Marmara in the Bakirköy district, the Ataköy Marina Hotel is only 8 km (5 miles) from Ataturk Airport. Facilities include tennis courts, swimming pool and meeting rooms. There is a shuttle bus to Sultanahmet 10 km (6 miles) away. *Sahilyolu • (0212) 560 41 10 • www.atakoymarinahotel.com.tr • $$$$$*

### 10 Hilton Hotel, Harbiye

Conveniently located for Taksim and the business districts, this grand hotel has 498 rooms, fitness centre, tennis courts, two pools, *hamam*, conference facilities and much more. *Cumhuriyet Cad • Map B5 • (0212) 315 60 00 • www.hilton.com • $$$$$*

*Note that all hotel price indications in this guide are given in US dollars, based on an exchange rate of 1TL (Turkish Lira): US $0.67*

Left **Hotel Empress Zöe** Centre **Blue House Hotel** Right **Yeşil Ev**

# Top 10 Characterful Hotels, Sultanahmet

### 1 Yeşil Ev
The 19 rooms in this restored mansion vary in size, but they all contain antiques and most face the garden. *Kabasakal Cad 5 • Map R5 • (0212) 517 67 86 • www.yesilev.com • $$$$*

### 2 Ayasofya Konakları
The first of the "special hotels" in Sultanahmet, this stretches along nine restored houses and has 64 rooms. The café or restaurant make a good rest point between Topkapı Palace and the Archaeological Museum. *Soğukçeşme Sok • Map R4 • (0212) 513 36 60 • www.ayasofyakonaklari.com • $$$*

### 3 Hotel Dersaadet
Its name means "place of felicity and beauty" – perfect for this Ottoman house at the foot of the hill behind Sultanahmet Square (the Hippodrome). There are superb views of the old city or the sea from all 17 rooms. *Küçük Ayasofya Cad, Kapıağası Sok 5 • Map Q6 • (0212) 458 07 60/1 • www.hoteldersaadet.com • $$$*

### 4 Hotel Empress Zöe
Old houses surround a lush garden and ruins of a 15th-century bath house at this delightful hotel, supposedly once the home of the Empress Zöe *(see p37)*. Its 25 rooms and suites are decorated in Turkish style. There is an informal bar service in the evenings. *Akbıyık Cad, Adliye Sok 10 • Map R5 • (0212) 518 43 60/25 04 • www.emzoe.com • $$$*

### 5 Blue House Hotel
This Wedgewood-blue hotel is in a quiet street behind the Arasta Bazaar, its relative calm broken only by the muezzin, and dervishes whirling in the restaurant opposite. All 27 rooms have superb views – the Blue Mosque (Sultan Ahmet Camii) seems close enough to touch. *Dalbastı Sok 14 • Map R5 • (0212) 638 90 10 • www.bluehouse.com.tr • $$$$*

### 6 Best Western Acropol Hotel
The 28 rooms in this restored Ottoman house have wooden floors and painted ceilings – but also wireless Internet and double glazing. The fifth-floor restaurant has fine views. Free airport transfers are offered. *Akbıyık Cad 25 • Map R5 • (0212) 638 90 21 • www.acropolhotel.com • $$$*

### 7 Hotel Kybele
Intimate, family-run and friendly, and a couple of steps from Divanyolu, this Aladdin's Cave of a hotel is a treasure trove of Turkish history, with hundreds of lamps and other Ottoman antiques decorating the public rooms, 16 bedrooms and garden. *Yerebatan Cad 35 • Map R4 • (0212) 511 77 66/7 • www.kybelehotel.com • $$$*

### 8 Arena Hotel
In an alley behind Sultanahmet Square, this was once the owner's home and is decorated with mementos. Most of the 27 rooms, including four suites, are spacious, with a sea view – and baths (unusual in many special hotels). *Küçükayasofya Mah, Şehit Mehmet Paşa Yokuşu, Uçler Hamam Sok 13–15 • Map P6 • (0212) 458 03 64 • www.arenahotel.com • $$$*

### 9 Sarı Konak Oteli
The owners of this 19-room hotel pride themselves on providing a "home from home". The café has 360° views, and breakfast is served in a Byzantine courtyard. A 10 per cent discount is given for cash payments. *Mimar Mehmet Ağa Cad 42–6 • Map R5 • (0212) 638 62 58 • www.sarikonak.com • $$$*

### 10 Sarnıç Hotel
This 21-room hotel behind the Blue Mosque has a lovely rooftop terrace restaurant. Guests can inspect the magnificent 5th-century Byzantine cistern (*sarnıç*) under the hotel. Turkish cookery classes are available. *Küçük Ayasofya Cad 26 • Map Q6 • (0212) 518 23 23 • www.sarnichotel.com • $$*

***Unless otherwise stated, all hotels accept credit cards, and have en-suite bathrooms, air conditioning and Internet access.***

Hotel Kariye, Edirnekapı

**Price Categories**

For a standard, double room per night (with breakfast if included), taxes and extra charges.

| | |
|---|---|
| $ | under $45 |
| $$ | $45–80 |
| $$$ | $80–180 |
| $$$$ | $180–300 |
| $$$$$ | over $300 |

# Top 10 Characterful Hotels Further Afield

## 1 Anemon Galata, Beyoğlu

This 27-room hotel in a restored Art Nouveau mansion is just a short walk from Beyoğlu's shopping and nightlife. *Büyük Hendek Cad 5, Kuledibi • Map F2 • (0212) 293 23 43 • www.anemonhotels.com • $$$$*

## 2 Antik Hotel

This comfortable hotel built around a 1,500-year-old water cistern has fine views over the Sea of Marmara and makes visitors feel very welcome. The cistern itself has been converted into a subterranean nightclub and is a popular party spot. *Ordu Cad, Darphane Sok 10 • Map M4 • (0212) 638 58 58 • www.antik-hotel.com • $$$*

## 3 Hotel Kariye, Edirnekapı

This late-19th-century wooden mansion has 27 rooms and suites (with modern amenities) and a garden overlooking the Golden Horn. *Kariye Camii Sok 6 • Map J3 • (0212) 534 84 14 • www.kariyeotel.com • $$$*

## 4 Barceló Saray, Beyazıt

A comfortable and stylish 96-room boutique hotel just a stone's throw from the Grand Bazaar, this is an ideal place for avid shoppers or for those wanting a change of pace while still being in the heart of the action. *Yeniçeriler Cad 85 • Map N4 • (0212) 458 98 00 • www.barcelosaray.com • $$$*

## 5 Vardar Palace Hotel, Taksim

The public rooms of this former palace (built in 1901 and converted to a hotel in 1989) retain some Seljuk-style decoration. There are 40 spacious bedrooms, fine views from the roof terrace, and a pleasant restaurant downstairs. *Sıraselviler Cad 16 • Map L4 • (0212) 252 2888 • www.vardarhotel.com • $$*

## 6 Eklektik Guesthouse, Galata

A funky guesthouse in a restored Ottoman house, this has seven rooms decorated in styles from 60s retro to colonial. *Kadribey Cikmazı 4, Serdari Ekrem Cad • Map F2 • (0212) 243 74 46 • www.eklektikgalata.com • $$*

## 7 Hotel Villa Zurich, Cihangir

A short walk from Taksim Square, the 42-room Villa Zurich has a breakfast terrace with Bosphorus views. *Akarsu Yokusu Cad 44/46 • Map G2 • (0212) 293 06 04 • www.hotelvillazurich.com • $$*

## 8 Sumahan Hotel, Çengelköy (Asian Side)

Magnificently converted from an old *rakı* distillery by its architect owners, the 18-room Sumahan on the Asian shore of the Bosphorus is fast getting a reputation as one of Istanbul's best small hotels. Perhaps not the best sightseeing base (transport can be difficult, although the hotel runs shuttle boats), it is ideal for a romantic break. *Kuleli Cad 51 • Map U4 • (0216) 422 80 00 • www.sumahan.com • $$$$$*

## 9 Turquhouse Boutique Hotel, Pierre Loti

The Turquhouse covers the whole hill behind the Pierre Loti Café, with superb views across the Golden Horn. It has 67 rooms (some triples and family rooms), in restored Ottoman houses. Most guests are Turkish. *Merkez Mahallesi İdris Köşkü Cad Eyüp, Pierre Loti Tepesi Tesisleri • Map A4 • (0212) 497 13 13 • www.turquhouse.com • $$$*

## 10 Bebek Hotel, Bosphorus

Long since one of the favourite drinking haunts of Istanbul high society, where they sipped their gin while admiring their floating palaces, this 21-room hotel has been updated. For a little chic luxury, this could well be ideal. The only drawback is heavy traffic heading back to the centre. *Cevdetpaşa Cad 34, Bebek • Map U4 • (0212) 358 20 00 • www.bebekhotel.com.tr • $$$$*

*Note that all hotel price indications in this guide are given in US dollars, based on an exchange rate of 1TL (Turkish Lira): US $0.67*

Left **Side Hotel & Pension** Centre **Apricot Hotel** Right **Büyük Londra**

# Top 10 Budget and Self-Catering

### 1 Naz Wooden House Inn, Sultanahmet

This wooden bed and breakfast is right in the heart of the old city. The seven imaginatively decorated rooms are very good value, while the roof terrace has views worth ten times the price. *Akbıyık Değirmeni Sok 7 • Map R6 • (0212) 516 71 30 • www.nazwoodenhouseinn.com • $*

### 2 Apricot Hotel, Sultanahmet

A restored Ottoman mansion with hardwood floors (and ceilings) and traditional furnishings, the Apricot Hotel has 24 rooms, six with either a Jacuzzi or a Turkish bath. Barbecues are held on the terrace in summer. *Amiral Tafdil Sok 18 • Map R5 • (0212) 638 16 58 • www.apricothotel.com • $*

### 3 Side Hotel & Pension, Sultanahmet

You can choose between a full-service hotel (half with air conditioning, half with fans), two self-catering apartments and a more basic pension (without air conditioning) – all side by side, and under the same management. You couldn't get closer to Haghia Sophia (Ayasofya), and the views from the roof are simply superb. *Utangaç Sok 20 • Map R5 • (0212) 517 22 82 • www.sidehotel.com • $$*

### 4 Büyük (Grand) Londra, Beyoğlu

Faded decadence at its most alluring, the Londra has been an atmospheric and economic place to stay ever since the early 1900s, attracting Ernest Hemingway and other not-so-famous writers since (and featuring in the Turkish hit film *Head On*). Some of the eccentrically decorated rooms overlook the Golden Horn; many have been renovated over the years. *Meşrutiyet Cad 53 • Map J5 • (0212) 245 06 70 • www.londrahotel.net • $$*

### 5 Galata Residence Hotel, Karaköy

The 15 apartments in this vast 19th-century mansion (formerly owned by the Camondo family) have their own kitchens, bathrooms, air conditioning and TV, and are cleaned daily. There's a bar in the basement and superb views from the rooftop restaurant. *Bankalar Cad, Felek Sok • Map F3 • (0212) 292 48 41 • www.galataresidence.com • $*

### 6 Hotel Sultanahmet, Sultanahmet

A popular budget choice on the main drag, the Sultanahmet does the basics well, with clean neat rooms and friendly staff. *Divanyolu Cad 20 • Map Q4 • (0212) 527 02 39 • www.hotelsultanahmet.com • $*

### 7 Istanbul Holiday Apartments

Each of these seven restored buildings – two near the Galata Tower, one in Cihangir, Sultanahmet, Taksim, Kabataş and one near Beşıktaş – offers several apartments sleeping 1 to 6 people. *Map F3, Map G2, Map C5 • (0212) 251 85 30 • www.istanbulholidayapartments.com • $$*

### 8 Hotel Bulvar Palace, Saraçhane

This is a great deal – a four-star hotel at budget prices. The location near the Grand Bazaar is good, and the 70 rooms and 10 suites are comfortable and well equipped. Free airport transfers thrown in on request. *Atatürk Bulvari 152 • Map D5 • (0212) 528 58 81 • www.hotelbulvarpalas.com • $$*

### 9 Şebnem Hotel, Sultanahmet

The Şebnem is a small, welcoming guesthouse, with 15 simply decorated rooms (including one triple and one family room). *Adliye Sok 1 • Map S5 • (0212) 517 66 23 • www.sebnemhotel.net • $*

### 10 Hotel the Pera Hill, Beyoğlu

The rooms are decent-sized, clean and basic. The location, just a few steps from Beyoğlu, is fabulous. *Meşrutiyet Cad 39 • Map J5 • (0212) 245 66 06 • www.hoteltheperahill.com • $*

*Unless otherwise stated, all hotels accept credit cards, and have en-suite bathrooms, air conditioning and Internet access.*

Splendid Palace, Büyükada (Princes' Islands)

**Price Categories**

| For a standard, double room per night (with breakfast if included), taxes and extra charges. | |
|---|---|
| $ | under $45 |
| $$ | $45–80 |
| $$$ | $80–180 |
| $$$$ | $180–300 |
| $$$$$ | over $300 |

# TOP 10 Staying Out of Town

### 1 Splendid Palace Hotel, Büyükada (Princes' Islands)

There are touches of Art Nouveau elegance in this very grand *belle époque* hotel, built in 1908 around a central courtyard. The 70 rooms and four suites all have balconies and wonderful views. *23 Nisan Cad 53 • (0216) 382 69 50 • www.splendidhotel.net • $$*

### 2 Merit Halki Palace, Heybeliada (Princes' Islands)

A beautifully restored old wooden house, the hotel offers lovely views across Heybeliada and the Sea of Marmara from the terrace restaurant, pool and balcony. *Refah Şehitleri Cad 94 • (0216) 351 00 25 • www.halkipalacehotel.com • $$$*

### 3 Anzac Hotel, Çanakkale

Travellers rave about the superb service at this small hotel, well placed for Troy and Gallipoli. There are 25 rooms, a restaurant and rooftop bar (in summer). *Saat Kulesi Meydanı 8 • (0286) 217 77 77 • www.anzachotel.com • $$*

### 4 Hotel Akol, Çanakkale

This modern high-rise hotel overlooking the waterfront in the town centre makes up in friendly efficiency what it lacks in atmosphere. It has a restaurant with good food but appalling decor, a rooftop bar, pool, and comfortable rooms with balconies and great views. *Kordon Boyu Cad • (0286) 217 94 56 • www.hotelakol.com • $$$*

### 5 Otantik Club Hotel, Bursa

A restored Ottoman merchant's house, this offers fresh air and greenery – a refuge from Bursa's crowded streets. The 29 spacious rooms have Ottoman-style decor. *Botanik Parkı, Soğanli • (0224) 211 32 80 • www.otantikclubhotel.com • $$$*

### 6 Safran Hotel, Bursa

This saffron-yellow converted Ottoman mansion with ten rooms has a somewhat functional, modern interior but could not be more conveniently located, right in the heart of the old city. It has a good restaurant with live music on some evenings. *Ortapazar Cad, Arka Sok 4, Tophane • (0224) 224 72 16/7 • www.safranotel.com • $*

### 7 Polka Country Hotel, Polonezköy

Paying homage to the village's central European roots, this is like a Polish hunting lodge, all heavy beams, polished wood, comfy armchairs and wall trophies. The facilities include 15 rooms, a café-bar, restaurant and sauna. This is a great place for a weekend escape to greenery and fresh air. *Cumhuriyet Yolu 20 • (0216) 423 32 20/1 • www.polkahotel.com • $$*

### 8 Iznik Foundation Guesthouse, Iznik

Owned by the people who have revived Iznik's distinguished tradition of ceramics, this basic but comfortable lakefront guesthouse, with only ten rooms, is friendly and convenient for exploring the town and the beach. *Sahil Yolu Vakıf Sok 13 • (0224) 757 60 25 • www.iznik.com • $$*

### 9 Rüstem Paşa Kervansaray, Edirne

This 16th-century inn was originally built by Sinan *(see p21)* for Rüstem Paşa, Grand Vizier to Suleyman I. It is still atmospheric, but don't expect luxury – it's fairly spartan. Thick stone walls make it cool in summer, cold in winter. The camel courtyard is a great spot to relax in. *Iki Kapılı Han Cad 57 • (0284) 212 61 19 • www.edirnekervansarayhotel.com • $$*

### 10 Fener Motel, Şile, Black Sea

This attractive modern low-rise resort hotel, near the beach, has 27 simply furnished stone-built rooms with verandas, and a campsite. *Balibey Mah, Aglayan Kaya Cad 18, Şile • (0216) 711 28 24 • www.fenermotel.com • $*

*Note that all hotel price indications in this guide are given in US dollars, based on an exchange rate of 1TL (Turkish Lira): US $0.67.*

# General Index

Page numbers in **bold** type refer to main entries.

# Acknowledgments


**The Author**
Melissa Shales is an award-winning travel writer. As author, contributor or editor, she has worked on more than 100 guide-books. She has written travel articles for many magazines, and was editor of *Traveller* magazine. During 2004–06 she was Chairman of the British Guild of Travel Writers.

The author would like to thank the following for their generosity, hard work and patience during the research of this book: the Turkish Tourist Office, particularly Joanna Marsh in London and İlginay Altuntaş in Istanbul; Emma Levine; and Victoria Gooch.

**Produced by** Coppermill Books, 55 Salop Road, London E17 7HS
**Editorial Director** Chris Barstow
**Designer** Ian Midson
**Copy Editor** Charles Phillips
**Editorial Consultant** Fay Franklin
**Proofreader** Antony Mason
**Fact-checker** Arzu Bölükbaşı
**Indexer** Hilary Bird
**Main Photographer** Antony Souter
**Additional Photography** Philip Entickna, Izzet Keribar, Linda Whitwam, Francesca Yorke
**Illustrator** Chapel Design & Marketing
**Maps** Simonetta Giori, Dominic Beddow (Draughtsman Ltd).

FOR DORLING KINDERSLEY
**Publisher** Douglas Amrine
**Publishing Manager** Christine Stroyan
**Senior Art Editor** Maite Lantaron
**Senior Cartographic Editor** Casper Morris
**DTP Designer** Natasha Lu
**Production Controller** Elizabeth Warman
**Revisions Team** Namrata Adhwaryu, Emma Anacootee, Şebnem Atılgan, Jennifer Barnes Eliot, Nadia Bonomally, Imogen Corke, Nicola Erdpresser, Anna Freiberger, Claire Jones, Batur Kızıltuğ, Shikha Kulkarni, Maite Lantaron, Hayley Maher, Helen Partington, Ellen Root, Preeti Singh, Sadie Smith, Conrad Van Dyk, Ajay Verma.

**Picture Credits**
Key: a-above; b-below/bottom; c-centre; f-far; l-left; r-right; t-top.

The publishers would like to thank the following individuals, companies and picture libraries for their kind permission to reproduce their photographs.

ALAMY IMAGES: Roger Cracknell 08/Greece 28crb; ATLANTIDE PHOTO TRAVEL: Massimo Borchi 30–31; AXIOM PHOTOGRAPHIC AGENCY: 54–5.

BRIDGEMAN ART LIBRARY: 32 bl, 33br. CAPAMARKA ENTERTAINMENT GROUP: 84tc; MAHMUT CEYLAN: 47t; 4CORNERS IMAGES: 64–5.

GALERI KAYSERI: 105TL; GETTY IMAGES/HULTON ARCHIVE: 32tr, 33cl; GÖKHAN KALI: 46t.

ISTANBUL DOORS GROUP: 50tr. İZZET KERİBAR: 100–101. ESBER METIN: 46br. AYLİN ÖZMETE: 46c; pera palace: 79tr.

SHUTTERSTOCK: Vitaly Titov and Maria Sidelnikova 104tc; SONIA HALLIDAY PHOTOGRAPHS: Topkapı Palace 11 bl; STAR GAZETE: MURAT DUZYOL 109TL.

TURKUAZOO: 48br.

# Phrase Book

## Pronunciation

Turkish uses a Roman alphabet of 29 letters: 8 vowels and 21 consonants. Letters that differ from the English alphabet are: c, pronounced "j" as in "jolly; ç, pronounced "ch" as in "church"; ğ, which lengthens the preceding vowel and is not pronounced; ı, pronounced "uh"; ö, pronounced "ur" (as in "further"); ş, pronounced "sh" as in "ship"; and ü, pronounced "ew" as in "few".

## In an Emergency

| | | |
|---|---|---|
| Help! | **İmdat!** | eem-**dat** |
| Call a doctor! | **Bir doktor çağrın!** | beer dok-**tor chah**-ruhn |
| Call an ambulance! | **Bir ambulans çağrın!** | beer am-boo-**lans chah**-ruhn |
| Call the police! | **Polis çağrın!** | po-**lees chah**-ruhn |
| Fire! | **Yangın!** | yan-**guhn** |
| Where is the nearest telephone/ hospital? | **En yakın telefon/ hastane nerede?** | en ya-**kuhn** teh-leh-**fon**/ has-ta-**neh neh**-reh-deh |

## Communication Essentials

| | | |
|---|---|---|
| Yes | **Evet** | eh-***vet*** |
| No | **Hayır** | h-'**eye**'-uhr |
| Thank you | **Teşekkür ederim** | teh-shek-**kewr eh**-deh-reem |
| Please | **Lütfen** | **lewt**-fen |
| Excuse me | **Affedersiniz** | **af**-feh-der-see-neez |
| Hello | **Merhaba** | **mer**-ha-ba |
| Goodbye | **Hoşça kalın** | hosh-**cha ka**-luhn |
| Morning | **Sabah** | sa-**bah** |
| Afternoon | **Öğleden sonra** | ur-leh-**den son**-ra |
| Evening | **Akşam** | ak-**sham** |
| Yesterday | **Dün** | dewn |
| Today | **Bugün** | **boo**-gewn |
| Tomorrow | **Yarın** | **ya**-ruhn |
| Here | **Burada** | **boo**-ra-da |
| There | **Şurada** | **shoo**-ra-da |
| What? | **Ne?** | neh |
| When? | **Ne zaman?** | **neh za**-man |
| Where? | **Nerede** | **neh**-reh-deh |

## Useful Phrases

| | | |
|---|---|---|
| Pleased to meet you | **Memnun oldum** | mem-**noon ol**-doom |
| Where is/are? | **nerede?** | **neh**-reh-deh |
| How far is it to? | **ne kadar uzakta?** | **neh ka**-dar oo-zak-ta |
| Do you speak English? | **İngilizce biliyor musunuz?** | een-gee-**leez**-jeh bee-**lee**-yor moo-soo-nooz? |
| I don't understand | **Anlamıyorum** | an-**la**-muh-yo-room |
| Can you help me? | **Bana yardım edebilir misiniz?** | ba-**na** yar-**duhm** eh-deh-bee-**leer** mee-see-neez? |
| I don't want | **istemiyorum** | ees-**teh**-mee-yo-room |

## Useful Words

| | | |
|---|---|---|
| big | **büyük** | bew-**yewk** |
| small | **küçük** | kew-**chewk** |
| hot | **sıcak** | suh-**jak** |
| cold | **soğuk** | soh-**ook** |
| good/well | **iyi** | ee-**yee** |
| bad | **kötü** | kur-**tew** |
| open | **acık** | a-**chuhk** |
| closed | **kapalı** | ka-pa-**luh** |
| left | **sol** | sol |
| right | **sağ** | saa |
| near | **yakın** | ya-**kuhn** |
| far | **uzak** | oo-**zak** |
| up | **yukarı** | yoo-ka-**ruh** |
| down | **aşağı** | a-shah-**uh** |
| early | **erken** | er-**ken** |
| late | **geç** | gech |
| toilets | **tuvaletler** | too-va-let-**ler** |

## Shopping

| | | |
|---|---|---|
| How much is this? | **Bu kaç lira?** | boo **kach** lee-ra |
| I would like | **istiyorum** | ees-**tee**-yo-room |
| Do you have? | **var mı?** | **var** muh? |
| Do you take credit cards? | **Kredi kartı kabul ediyor musunuz?** | **kreh**-dee **kar**-tuh ka-**bool** eh-**dee**-yor moo-soo-nooz? |
| What time do you open/ close? | **Saat kaçta açılıyor/ kapanıyor?** | Sa-**at** kach-**ta** a-chuh-**luh**-yor/ ka-pa-**nuh**-yor |
| this one | **bunu** | boo-**noo** |
| that one | **şunu** | shoo-**noo** |
| expensive | **pahalı** | pa-ha-**luh** |
| cheap | **ucuz** | oo-**jooz** |
| size (clothes) | **beden** | beh-**den** |
| size (shoes) | **numara** | noo-ma-**ra** |
| white | **beyaz** | bay-**yaz** |
| black | **siyah** | see-**yah** |
| red | **kırmızı** | kuhr-muh-**zuh** |
| yellow | **sarı** | sa-**ruh** |
| green | **yeşil** | yeh-**sheel** |
| blue | **mavi** | ma-**vee** |
| brown | **kahverengi** | kah-**veh**-ren-gee |
| shop | **dükkan** | dewk-**kan** |
| That's my last offer | **Daha fazla veremem** | da-**ha faz**-la veh-**reh**-mem |

## Types of Shop

| | | |
|---|---|---|
| antiques shop | **antikacı** | an-**tee**-ka-juh |
| bakery | **fırın** | fuh-**ruhn** |
| bank | **banka** | **ban**-ka |
| book shop | **kitapçı** | kee-tap-**chuh** |
| cake shop | **pastane** | pas-ta-**neh** |
| chemist's/ pharmacy | **eczane** | ej-za-**neh** |
| greengrocer's | **manav** | ma-**nav** |
| leather shop | **derici** | deh-ree-**jee** |
| market/bazaar | **çarşı/pazar** | char-**shuh**/pa-**zar** |
| newsstand | **gazeteci** | ga-**zeh**-teh-jee |
| post office | **postane** | pos-ta-**neh** |
| shoe shop | **ayakkabıcı** | 'eye'-**yak**-ka-buh-juh |
| supermarket | **süpermarket** | sew-per-mar-**ket** |
| tailor | **terzi** | ter-**zee** |
| travel agency | **seyahat acentesi** | say-ya-**hat** a-jen-teh-**see** |

## Sightseeing

| | | |
|---|---|---|
| castle | **hisar** | hee-**sar** |
| church | **kilise** | kee-**lee**-seh |
| mosque | **cami** | **ja**-mee |
| museum | **müze** | **mew**-zeh |
| palace | **saray** | sar-'**eye**' |
| park | **park** | park |
| square | **meydan** | may-**dan** |
| information office | **danışma bürosu** | da-nuhsh-**mah bew**-ro-soo |
| Turkish bath | **hamam** | ha-**mam** |

## Transport

| | | |
|---|---|---|
| airport | **havalimanı** | ha-**va**-lee-ma-nuh |
| bus/coach | **otobüs** | o-to-**bewss** |
| bus stop | **otobüs durağı** | o-to-**bewss** doo-**ra**-uh |
| coach station | **otogar** | o-to-**gar** |
| dolmuş | **dolmuş** | dol-**moosh** |
| fare | **ücret** | ewj-**ret** |
| ferry | **vapur** | va-**poor** |

| | | |
|---|---|---|
| sea bus | **deniz otobüsü** | deh-**neez** o-to-**bew**-sew |
| station | **istasyon** | ees-tas-**yon** |
| taxi | **taksi** | **tak**-see |
| ticket | **bilet** | bee-**let** |
| ticket office | **bilet gişesi** | bee-**let** gee-sheh-**see** |
| timetable | **tarife** | ta-ree-**feh** |

## Staying in a Hotel

| | | |
|---|---|---|
| Do you have a vacant room? | **Boş odanız var mı?** | bosh o-da-**nuhz** **var** muh? |
| double room | **iki kişilik bir oda** | ee-**kee** kee-shee-**leek** beer o-**da** |
| twin room | **çift yataklı bir oda** | **cheeft** ya-**tak**-luh beer o-**da** |
| for one person | **tek kişilik** | **tek** kee-shee-**leek** |
| room with a bath | **banyolu bir oda** | **ban**-yo-loo beer o-**da** |
| shower | **duş** | doosh |
| porter | **komi** | ko-**mee** |
| key | **anahtar** | a-nah-**tar** |
| room service | **oda servisi** | o-**da** ser-vee-**see** |
| I have a reservation | **Rezervasyonum var** | reh-zer-vas-yo-**noom** var |

## Eating Out

| | | |
|---|---|---|
| I want to reserve a table | **Bir masa ayırtmak istiyorum** | beer **ma**-sa 'eye'-uhrt-**mak** ees-**tee**-yo-room |
| The bill please | **Hesap lütfen** | heh-**sap** **lewt**-fen |
| I am a vegetarian | **Et yemiyorum** | et **yeh**-mee-yo-room |
| restaurant | **lokanta** | lo-**kan**-ta |
| waiter | **garson** | gar-**son** |
| menu | **yemek listesi** | ye-**mek** **lees**-teh-see |
| wine list | **şarap listesi** | sha-**rap** **lees**-teh-see |
| breakfast | **kahvaltı** | kah-val-**tuh** |
| lunch | **öğle yemeği** | ur-**leh** yeh-meh-**ee** |
| dinner | **akşam yemeği** | ak-**sham** yeh-meh-**ee** |
| starter | **meze** | **meh**-zeh |
| main course | **ana yemek** | a-**na** yeh-**mek** |
| dessert | **tatlı** | tat-**luh** |
| rare | **az pişmiş** | **az** peesh-meesh |
| well done | **iyi pişmiş** | ee-**yee** peesh-meesh |
| glass | **bardak** | bar-**dak** |
| bottle | **şişe** | shee-**sheh** |
| knife | **bıçak** | buh-**chak** |
| fork | **çatal** | cha-**tal** |
| spoon | **kaşık** | ka-**shuhk** |

## Menu Decoder

| | | |
|---|---|---|
| **balık** | ba-**luhk** | fish |
| **bira** | **bee**-ra | beer |
| **bonfile** | **bon**-fee-leh | fillet steak |
| **buz** | booz | ice |
| **çay** | ch-'eye' | tea |
| **çorba** | chor-**ba** | soup |
| **dana eti** | da-**na** eh-**tee** | veal |
| **dondurma** | don-door-**ma** | ice cream |
| **ekmek** | ek-**mek** | bread |
| **et** | et | meat |
| **fırında** | fuh-ruhn-**da** | roast |
| **fıstık** | fuhs-**tuhk** | pistachio nuts |
| **gazoz** | ga-**zoz** | fizzy drink |
| **hurma** | hoor-ma | dates |
| **içki** | eech-**kee** | alcohol |
| **incir** | een-**jeer** | figs |
| **ızgara** | uhz-**ga**-ra | charcoal grilled |
| **kahve** | kah-**veh** | coffee |
| **kara biber** | ka-**ra** bee-**ber** | black pepper |
| **karışık** | ka-ruh-**shuhk** | mixed |
| **kaymak** | k-'eye'-**mak** | cream |
| **kıyma** | kuhy-**ma** | minced meat |
| **köfte** | kurf-**teh** | meatballs |
| **kuzu eti** | koo-**zoo** eh-**tee** | lamb |
| **lokum** | lo-**koom** | Turkish delight |
| **maden suyu** | ma-**den** soo-**yoo** | mineral water (fizzy) |
| **meyve suyu** | may-**veh** soo-**yoo** | fruit juice |
| **midye** | **meed**-yeh | mussels |
| **patlıcan** | pat-luh-**jan** | aubergine |
| **peynir** | pay-**neer** | cheese |
| **pilav** | pee-**lav** | rice |
| **piliç** | pee-**leech** | roast chicken |
| **şarap** | sha-**rap** | wine |
| **şeker** | sheh-**ker** | sugar |
| **su** | soo | water |
| **süt** | sewt | milk |
| **tavuk** | ta-**vook** | chicken |
| **tereyağı** | teh-**reh**-yah-uh | butter |
| **tuz** | tooz | salt |
| **yoğurt** | yoh-**urt** | yoghurt |
| **yumurta** | yoo-moor-**ta** | egg |
| **zeytinyağı** | zay-**teen**-yah-uh | olive oil |

## Numbers

| | | |
|---|---|---|
| 0 | **sıfır** | **suh**-fuhr |
| 1 | **bir** | beer |
| 2 | **iki** | ee-**kee** |
| 3 | **üç** | ewch |
| 4 | **dört** | durt |
| 5 | **beş** | besh |
| 6 | **altı** | al-**tuh** |
| 7 | **yedi** | yeh-**dee** |
| 8 | **sekiz** | seh-**keez** |
| 9 | **dokuz** | doh-**kooz** |
| 10 | **on** | on |
| 11 | **on bir** | **on** beer |
| 12 | **on iki** | **on** ee-kee |
| 13 | **on üç** | **on** ewch |
| 14 | **on dört** | **on** durt |
| 15 | **on beş** | **on** besh |
| 16 | **on altı** | **on** al-tuh |
| 17 | **on yedi** | **on** yeh-dee |
| 18 | **on sekiz** | **on** seh-keez |
| 19 | **on dokuz** | **on** doh-kooz |
| 20 | **yirmi** | yeer-**mee** |
| 21 | **yirmi bir** | yeer-mee **beer** |
| 30 | **otuz** | o-**tooz** |
| 40 | **kırk** | kuhrk |
| 50 | **elli** | eh-**lee** |
| 60 | **altmış** | alt-**muhsh** |
| 70 | **yetmiş** | yet-**meesh** |
| 80 | **seksen** | sek-**sen** |
| 90 | **doksan** | dok-**san** |
| 100 | **yüz** | yewz |
| 200 | **iki yüz** | ee-**kee** yewz |
| 1,000 | **bin** | been |
| 100,000 | **yüz bin** | **yewz** been |
| 1,000,000 | **bir milyon** | **beer** meel-**yon** |

## Time

| | | |
|---|---|---|
| one minute | **bir dakika** | **beer** da-**kee**-ka |
| one hour | **bir saat** | **beer** **sa**-at |
| half an hour | **yarım saat** | ya-**ruhm** **sa**-at |
| day | **gün** | gewn |
| week | **hafta** | haf-**ta** |
| month | **ay** | 'eye' |
| year | **yıl** | yuhl |
| Sunday | **pazar** | pa-**zar** |
| Monday | **pazartesi** | pa-**zar**-teh-see |
| Tuesday | **salı** | sa-**luh** |
| Wednesday | **çarşamba** | char-sham-**ba** |
| Thursday | **perşembe** | per-shem-**beh** |
| Friday | **cuma** | joo-**ma** |
| Saturday | **cumartesi** | joo-**mar**-teh-see |

# Selected Street Index